This Boy's Heart

'John's memoir is a thing of beauty. I adored it. I could hear his gentle voice telling every story. Were Cork and Ireland ever more gorgeously described? Through a decade of his boyhood, he tells the story of the life of a country, and of a family, with deep love and affection. Full of heart and warmth and humour, this is a book to lift your spirits.'

– DONAL RYAN

Gill Books
Hume Avenue
Park West
Dublin 12
www.gillbooks.ie

Gill Books is an imprint of M.H. Gill and Co.

© John Creedon 2024

978 1 8045 8048 6

Designed by Sarah McCoy
Edited by Catherine Gough
Copyedited by Esther Ní Dhonnacha
Endpaper map by Bex Sheridan
Printed and bound by Scandbook, Sweden
This book is typeset in Freight Text.

The paper used in this book comes from the wood pulp of sustainably managed forests.

All rights reserved.
No part of this publication may be copied, reproduced or transmitted in any form or by any means, without written permission of the publishers.

A CIP catalogue record for this book is available from the British Library.

5 4 3 2 1

This Boy's Heart

Scenes from an Irish childhood

JOHN CREEDON

John Creedon

Gill Books

Contents

Author's Note	*vii*
Introduction	1
Where the Sacred Heart Is	7
A Rogue Is Born	15
Gentle as the Fawn	25
Sex on the Wall	37
Blessed Martin	58
Family Pass	69
Rite of Passage	77
A Neighbour's Child	89
The Sound of One Hand Slapping	98
Putting the Fist into Pacifist	110
Ballybunion	118
Away with the Manger	136
Farmed Out	144
Tom the Traveller	161
Mrs Manley	174
Saints, Sinners and Santy	184
Aunty Theresa	198
Eurovision	212
One to Stop	230
The Orange Curtain	237
My Vocation	244
The Formica Bar	258
The Donkey Derby	268
Riding off into the Sunset	282
Postscript	*292*
Glossary of Terms	*293*
Acknowledgements	*295*

Author's Note

These scenes are drawn from one decade of my life – 1960 to 1970 – and are set between the intense exotica of city-centre streets and the open meadows of the Irish countryside.

Most of us, I expect, will have experienced or witnessed injustice and cruelty during childhood. I know I have. However, I was spared the deep trauma visited upon so many children around the world. For the most part, my formative years were carefree. I grew up amongst a loving family in a country I dearly love. So it is with deep humility and gratitude that I offer this personal memoir.

I'm mindful that childhood is a shared experience and my beloved siblings, cousins and childhood friends will all have their own stories to tell. Many of them already have. So, in the spirit of an tAthair Peadar Ó Laoghaire, who wrote *Mo Scéal Féin*, this is my own story. I share it with deep affection and recollection.

Some names and locations have been changed.

ooo

Childhood is a fragile thing, and this book is dedicated to my grandchildren: Bonnie, Brodie, Chloe, Cody, Ella, Fiadh, Lucie, Mollie and Rosie.

Introduction

With deep affection and recollection
I often think of the Shandon bells,
Whose sound so wild would, in days of childhood,
Fling round my cradle their magic spells.
On this I ponder, where'er I wander,
And thus grow fonder, sweet Cork, of thee,
With thy bells of Shandon,
That sound so grand on
The pleasant waters of the river Lee.

– Excerpt from 'The Bells Of Shandon',
Francis Sylvester Mahony ('Father Prout'), 1804–1866

I am in my sixty-fifth year and in the garden with my hero, Laoch, the warrior robin. I've been passing him sweet treats, mouth to beak, to the amusement of my grandchildren. In he comes again like a hummingbird, reverse flapping as he lowers the landing gear. We're both in slow motion as he hovers. Two scaly claws extend, tiny drumsticks flex and retract like shock absorbers. Then, in one neat precision snatch, a dainty beak accepts the gift between my lips and, using my chin as a launch pad, he pushes off and away.

The show is over now and the children have galloped off, back indoors. Further along the northern slopes of the city, someone is playing 'The Banks of My Own Lovely Lee' on the ancient bells of Shandon steeple. The soft tolling of the bells summons up that minor-key melancholia of childhood memory.

A layer of ennui softly lands on the already textured soundtrack of the city below me: birdsong, children in a playground, a faint and distant ice-cream van, and an ambulance away out on the Southside.

Apart from the 13 years I spent in Dublin, I have lived my life under Shandon's bells. When I was a small child, my bedroom window was within both earshot and eyeshot of the steeple, and on waking from a bad dream or feeling anxious about unfinished homework, Shandon's quarter-hour bell would comfort me. With Seán Bunny, my bedtime huggy-pal, tucked under my arm, I'd lie there listening. Eventually, my attention would settle on the out-of-tune, slow notes as they reverberated and faded, drawing me with them through the sleep portal.

Although we attended the nearby Roman Catholic church, St Mary's on Pope's Quay, we had huge affection for Shandon. Its giant pepper-cannister tower sports the Cork colours. Two sides are faced in old red sandstone and the other two in white limestone, all topped by a huge golden weather vane in the shape of a salmon, known locally as 'De Goldie

Fish'. Each of the tower's four giant clocks display a different time, which earned it the nickname 'The Four-faced Liar'. But, as a neighbour of ours once observed, 'Sure, if they all told the right time, we'd only need the one clock.'

The beautiful sadness of Abel Rudhall's bells first rang out from St Anne's, Shandon, to announce the marriage of Catherine Dornan to Henry Harding on the morning of 7 December 1752. Millions of Corkonians have since come and gone, but Shandon still holds the high ground and continues to serve those of the Anglican tradition.

While the repetition of the Rosary was my Catholic mantra, the Protestants provided my meditation bell.

Even now, in the garden, those chimes lull me into reflection. When asked for our earliest childhood memories, most of us, I expect, have vague, grainy home-movie images in our heads. Science would say that many of us can recall events from as early as two and a half years of age. But how do we know that a memory is a genuine eyewitness account of an event? Perhaps we are actually recalling a well-polished story, memorised from the telling and retelling of others? Family folklore is prone to exaggeration and colouring. I can visualise events that occurred before I was even born, but I'm searching now for fragments of real memoir.

For instance, there's a photograph of my brother Don's Confirmation and I'm not in it. I vaguely remember that I was sulking and refused to be in the photograph. I recall the gravel beneath me as I waddled away from the group.

There's also a short, blurry memory of being in the yard of the Munster Hotel across the road from our house, where my friend Jimmy Corbridge lived before his family moved to Wales. His dad was a Welshman and chief engineer on the old *Innisfallen*, which ploughed the waves from Cork to Fishguard. I clearly remember sailing with my older sisters Eugenia and Geraldine to visit the Corbridge family. Eugenia and I, giddy with the excitement of sailing at night, kept interrupting Geraldine, who stood outside our cabin being chatted up by a handsome young steward.

Truly momentous events will sometimes occur, unbidden, in an otherwise ordinary life. I have a vivid recollection of seeing John F. Kennedy in June 1963 as his motorcade swept past the top of our street. The entire neighbourhood had gathered on Patrick's Hill to see the handsome American president and his tan. I distinctly remember being hooshed onto a low roof by some older friends, and from there onto a dormer window, then hoisted by my arms onto the roof of the Provincial Bank of Ireland, the perfect vantage point to witness history. Little did JFK, or the rest of us gathered on that hill, know the fate that awaited him in Dallas a few months later.

I still have a blurry recollection of the day he died. I can't actually remember what I was doing or who else was in the kitchen, but I do remember my mam turned down the shop lights and pushed out the shop door. My dad turned up the wireless and looked worriedly from my mother to the wireless and back again. I wasn't quite six yet, so I had no idea what this would mean for all of us. I was confused that someone would shoot such a nice man with his lovely smile, white teeth and American tan. It was as if the world had momentarily stopped turning and we had entered a vacuum, until Mam and Dad would try to make sense of it for us.

I'm roused from my reverie by the sound of my grandchildren coming back out to the garden to say goodbye. Loads of hugs and they're gone. However, the encounter with my own inner child lingers. I realise the boy within has so much he really wants to say. Maybe I haven't listened to him as much as he would have liked. Maybe nobody did, or could, for that matter. But the boy and myself have the rest of the day to ourselves, so we strike off for an amble along *Bóithrín na Smaointe* and back by Memory Lane.

At times, I take him by the hand, but mostly he's running along beside me, talking nineteen to the dozen. As the Shandon bells reverberate and fade, we're off ... wandering the streets of 1960s Cork in search of adventure. Back to a time when my father could skip across a bog carrying three children in his arms. A time when my mother would suppress a giggle as she taught us to waltz around the kitchen with a sweeping brush – one-two-three, one-two-three. A time when this boy's heart was as light as the wild winds that blow.

Where the Sacred Heart Is

'Hiren the wireless!'

'No! Don't! Lowern it!'

'Will ye get up?!'

Reveille in the Creedon household followed the exact same pattern every school morning. The bugle boy, my dad, was first up to attend to the overnight deliveries. He unlocked the shop door at 6 a.m., dragged in the crates of milk and bundles of newspapers, and turned the 'Open' sign to face the world. That sign only ever faced the other way for five hours a day.

Dad would switch on the kettle and the big radio set on either side of the gold-framed Sacred Heart picture in the kitchen and let them both warm up. Then he'd pop upstairs and give my mother a shout so that she could take over when he was gone to work. In between domestic duties, Dad would serve the first few customers, usually other dads rushing for the Ford and Dunlop factories down the docks.

At precisely 7.30 a.m., five sharp pips would emanate from the extension speaker on the third-floor landing. You see, apart from the wire at the back of the kitchen radio that served as an aerial, my father, an ingenious man, had attached yet another wire to the wireless, as it was curiously called. This cable was tacked discreetly beside the lino and rubber nosing cover on the steps of the stairs. It ran all the way to the speaker on the landing windowsill on the top floor outside my sisters' bedrooms. The speaker was housed in its own little mahogany box with fancy holes at the front to let the sound out. It looked like it belonged on a church wall, but it sat on that windowsill for decades. The knob on the side said 'Vol' and there were two little lines: one read 'Min', the other read 'Max'. But no matter how you twiddled it, the vol was always at max. And it worked – the Creedons always had a good school attendance record. Radio Éireann, above in Dublin, was now in on the act, calling the nation to rise up with 'O'Donnell Abú', aptly described as 'a rousing march'. It certainly put the heart crossways in the two dozen souls sleeping under our roof.

It was a particularly big roof as it spanned two conjoined three-storey houses, each with its own shopfront. There was a small yard behind one house and a large extension behind the other. The extension was built by 'Johnny the Builder' when I was a toddler, and it provided extra bedrooms and two bathrooms. All told, there were only 12 bedrooms, so at times it could be a little cramped.

There was Mam and Dad and their 12 children. Norah, Carol Ann, Constance, Geraldine, Vourneen, Don, Rosaleen, Marie-Thérèse and Eugenia were all doing just grand until number 10 – Baby John –

arrived in November 1958. They still call me Baby John. Miss Healy and Margaret O'Sullivan, who worked in the shop, also lived with us, as did Aunty Theresa and sometimes Aunty Martha, my mother's sisters. There was also a menagerie of dogs, cats and, at various times, a budgie, a hen, a piglet, a pigeon with a broken wing, and a hedgehog my dad found outside the shop door one morning.

There was also room on the far side of the house for two bedsits, home to the most colourful characters my mother could source from the classified ads in the *Cork Examiner*. There was Joey Connors, an American journalist, who wrote for *Time Life*, amongst others. You could hear Joey click-clacking away on his typewriter all day and into the wee small hours. He was tiny and wore a little hat, and he chain-smoked Lucky Strike cigarettes, which my mother would order in to the shop especially for him. With or without his glasses, he squinted. It was like having our very own Mr Magoo, and I loved calling around to visit Joey's bedsit. He wouldn't stop smoking or click-clacking for anyone, but with a cigarette dangling from one corner of his lip and his neck craning forwards to examine his own words on the typing paper as it emerged from the roller, he'd tell me all about America, communists, Steinbeck, Kerouac, Elvis and Martin Luther King Jr. He could type and talk at the same time, so he fitted right in with the chatterbox Creedons. Joey died in 1970 while on his way to Shannon Airport to cover President Richard Nixon's visit to Ireland.

Dr Nguryganda lived on the floor above Joey. He was from Kampala in Uganda, and he wasn't really a doctor. He was actually a dentistry student at UCC, but my mother insisted we refer to him as Dr Nguryganda to give him 'the ole boost', as my father would call it. He was handsome, like a young Sidney Poitier, and he wore skinny suits.

I remember my mother asking him about racism. It was a new word for me, but I distinctly remember him saying that some people had been cruel to him when he was studying in England. He recalled bringing a bag of washing to his local laundrette in London when some woman told him he should throw himself into the washing machine too. My mother was mortified to hear such a thing and I was cross. He said Irish people stared at him, but had not been nasty to him ... yet.

I might well have been the first. One day, three African nuns, who were probably also studying at UCC, called to our shop looking for Dr Nguryganda. I was told to bring them around to the side door that led up to the bedsits. I did, and then decided to spy on them. I watched that hall door all day, and the nuns never came out. By mid-afternoon, a horrific smell was coming from the bedsit. It was as if someone was boiling something that was gone off. It was clear to me that Dr Nguryganda was, in fact, a cannibal and that he had the three nuns tied together, boiling in a big pot. I tried telling my mother but she wouldn't believe me, so I had no choice but to burst into the bedsit and check.

Using the tried and trusted elements of surprise and confusion, I swept the bedsit door open and was in like a one-man SWAT team, lobbing a verbal smoke-grenade ahead of me to confuse them, 'Hello! Hello! Doctor Nguryganda, your *Daily Telegraph* has arrived below in the shop. Will I bring it up or will you ...?'

There they were – Dr Nguryganda and the nuns chomping away at their dinner. For a little boy, this was a traumatic introduction to garlic.

Dr Nguryganda and myself went on to become great friends. At my mother's insistence, I was his guide on a trip to Killarney, 60 miles away in County Kerry. I was only a small child and he was from Uganda, so neither of us knew the roads. However, we did manage to get the 6 miles to Blarney and back.

I was also his guest on a few trips to the Opera House to see the Cork comedy revue *Summer Revels*. I felt like royalty, with all those eyes following us as we crossed the plush carpet of the lobby of the theatre, me, my exotic guest, and our box of Maltesers. Panto dames Paddy Comerford and Billa O'Connell swaggered across the stage dressed as two old ladies from the city lanes having a right old barney. Billa, standing with his hands on his hips, whined, 'C'mere, gurl. If I spots you lookin' at my Tone-ee with dat guzz eye of yours again, I'll break every bone in your corset!' I wondered if Dr Nguryganda could make any sense of it, but he laughed in all the right places, so I think he enjoyed it.

ooo

Our shop, the Inchigeelagh Dairy, began as a retail outlet in the city for my grandfather's butter and egg business in Inchigeelagh. My father's Aunt Julia ran the shop on Devonshire Street until she retired and my father took over. Dad's older brother and best friend, my Uncle John, took the reins from Grandad in Inchigeelagh and ran the family hotel, shop, post office and milling business with his wife, Gretta, and their 14 children.

Devonshire Street was one side of a city block. Most of the buildings were hundreds of years old and included all manner of shops, pubs, family homes, flats, a bank, a hotel and an undertaker's. Just around the corner was McKenzie's agricultural suppliers with its shuffling queue of horses, donkeys and carts.

Because there were so many churches and schools in the city centre, our streets seemed to be full of nuns and priests and Brothers. We knew all the uniforms: Capuchins from Holy Trinity wore brown habits, the Ursuline nuns wore black with big wimples, other nuns wore navy-blue, and the Dominicans from Pope's Quay wore white robes with black outer garments. At the time, Ireland was producing huge numbers of both clergy and children. While the clergy concerned themselves with the rites of Rome, we children were more focused on the right to roam.

More often than not, we just took off and knocked on the front door of our latest best friend. If asked, I would simply tell my parents, 'I'm goin' out,' and run for it. Despite dire warnings, I'd often go missing and spend the afternoon on a high stool in any one of a dozen pubs or betting offices nearby. I'd while away the hours drinking raza (raspberry cordial and water) or tea, listening to the old fellas talking about dogs, hurling and the price of the pint. I still love the company of old people, but as I grow older myself, there seems to be less and less of them.

On our street alone, we had Granda Carr, who fought in World War I; Mr McAuliffe, a steeplejack who knew no fear; Johnny the Congo, who fought in Africa with the UN; Ned Ring the blacksmith; the Drummer Boy, who sang at Covent Garden; and Louie Angelini, a Scottish bookmaker with an Italian name.

It was a colourful community. Up the street we had Armenian Christians, a Presbyterian church and a Baptist community. At one point, an American family of coeliacs moved into a rented house up the hill. My mother ordered special bread to the shop for them. I never knew their surname, but because everyone just referred to them as 'the coeliacs', I assumed they were a religious group like all the others.

Most adults were addressed as Mr or Mrs. Our shop assistant of 20 years was known as Miss Healy, which I believed to be her Christian name. For years, I just assumed her full name was Misshealy Creedon. I nearly fell out of my stand when she showed me a postcard she received. It was addressed to a Miss Brigid Healy, whoever she was. Really, you could not be up to adults.

I was gone all day and would only return home to regale my parents with mimicry and tales of the carry-on. Then, when they weren't looking, I'd be gone again. The world was my oyster and Cork was my stage. It had a cast of thousands and a set made of open doors.

A Rogue Is Born

I greet you proud Iveleary's sons and daughters fair and true.
Assembled at the South End Club old friendships to renew.
This annual opportunity I'm loth to let it pass.
Ere I recite a tale tonight on my Inchigeela Lass.

– Excerpt from 'My Inchigeela Lass', thought to be written by Seán Ó Tuathaigh and composed by Jim Cooney

On 18 March 1919, my father, Connie Patrick Creedon, crash-landed onto his parents' bedroom floor. 'I slid along the lino and when I finally came to a halt, I gathered my senses, had one good look around me, and with my two little arms aloft, I declared, "Inchigeelagh! Thank you, God! Thank you!"'

At least, that's what he told me, anyway.

Unlike my dad, who witnessed his own birth in all its pain and elation, I cannot recall the day I landed at the Bon Secours hospital on College Road, Cork. I was told I was born on 4 November 1958, but I discovered recently that it was actually 3 November. Now, it may just have been a long labour, as I was huge. My sister Norah claims I was 12lbs at birth. Even in the new money that's still 5.44kg: a fine-sized turkey or two healthy babies. I sometimes wonder if that's it – maybe I'm actually a set of twins who never shut up.

But I do remember the day I first realised that my dad was 40 years older than me. It was the day of my Confirmation. I was 10, the youngest boy in the Confirmation class, and my father was dropping me off at the North cathedral. As he turned to leave, a schoolfriend's dad spotted him and enquired, 'How'ru, Connie?'

'Erra, only average, Tommy. *Cuíosach gan a bheith maíteach, mar a dhearfá.*' (Average without being actually sick, as they say.)

'Why? What's wrong with you, old stock?'

'Yerra, the usual. AND I hit the big five-oh today.'

'Jaysus, are you fifty, Connie?'

'I am, and 'tis downhill all the way to the grave from here on in.'

He was right, it was downhill all the way to the graveyard from the cathedral, but I had no idea before this moment that my dad was dying. I mean, we had been planning for my Confirmation, not his funeral. Yet there he was, hurrying away to die.

Inside, we lined up to get a clatter across the face from Bishop Connie Lucey. As we shuffled towards the front of the queue, I discreetly leaned towards my best friend, Tony Bullman, and whispered, 'My father's going to die!'

'SHHH!' spat a parent behind me.

Shortly afterwards, I got the clatter and became a strong and perfect Christian.

As it turns out, my dad did eventually die and we did carry him downhill all the way to his final resting place. However, that came a full 30 years later, when I was 40 and he was just a few weeks short of 80. Despite a little rust in the hips and ankles, my dad clocked up his fair share of miles in his fourscore years. He began, aged 15, driving Model TT Ford trucks for his father's mill in Inchigeelagh, before becoming a bus driver for CIÉ in Cork City.

My grandfather, Cornelius Creedon, an industrious man, was a native Irish-speaker who left Oileán Eidhneach (Island of the Ivy)/Béal Átha an Ghaorthaidh (Mouth of the Stream in a Thorny Place) in the late 1800s and headed for Butte, Montana. He worked there as a copper miner before returning to Ireland with a bag of money to marry my grandmother, Norah Cotter, on 18 April 1912. Norah was the postmistress in the village of Inse Geimhleach (Inchigeelagh) on the eastern end of Loch Allua, where the lake narrows to become the River Lee again before picking up pace on its journey to Cork Harbour and out to sea. Within a few years, Con and Norah's household included four sons, the village post office, a shop, a mill, some trucks and a small hotel in the village. The area was a *breac-Gaeltacht* (speckled Gaeltacht), where some households spoke Irish and others spoke English. Growing up behind the counter of the post office, my father, the youngest of the family, was fluent in both.

My dad always ate his food with relish – sometimes Yorkshire relish, other times just plain enthusiasm relish. I was often transfixed by a dimple on the side of his forehead that went in and out as his mandible chomped away on a pig's head or a big bowl of tripe and drisheen that had been boiled in milk with a knob of butter. He would add a few taps of the small drum of Saxa white pepper that never strayed too far from our kitchen table. Having grown up in a hotel popular with English anglers, where pheasant, venison, wild trout and salmon were staples, my dad was a connoisseur. He often regaled us with the story of a less erudite guest at the hotel who, when offered ox tongue by the waitress, baulked at the idea and replied, 'I couldn't possibly eat something that came out of an animal's mouth. I'll just have an egg instead.' Charming!

With the move to Cork City to attend secondary school, my father's taste for the exotic deepened. Living with his Aunt Julia in the Inchigeelagh Dairy on Devonshire Street provided young Connie Pa with an opportunity to dive into the delights of the city centre. The streets of 1930s Cork bustled with trams and horse-drawn trailers laden with barrels of porter from Murphy's Brewery, Thompson's cakes,

Hadji Bey's Turkish delight, corned beef, spiced beef, offal, fresh coffee and blended teas ... all produced within a few steps of our front door.

Connie Pa sucked the marrow out of life as if it were a leg of lamb. I can still see him with a tea towel flicked over one shoulder, hopping between serving customers in the shop and buttering mountains of brown bread for us, with the daily observation 'I feed my men well!' The tradition prevails. I never serve as much as a bowl of cereal to a guest without issuing the same salute to my own generosity.

Dad tipped the scales at 20 stone and he'd charm the birds from the trees. He was a swashbuckler, handsome and broad shouldered, a hurler, a hunter and a champion angler. As well as English and Irish, he spoke Classical Greek, Latin and Hainakatina, a language he created himself as a sort of shortcut to the word he was actually trying to think of. He would ask for a 'coo-jack-a-swivvey' as a generic term for the next tool he needed from the toolbox. If nature called while in company, he'd enquire if there was a 'conswilly' in the house. In a less affluent home, where the convenience might be outdoors, he'd probably ask for the 'tinny shed', the 'fowl house' or whatever other notion popped into his head.

A retired CIÉ man once told me about an occasion when some bus drivers were chatting as they finished up their shift for the day. It was

Christmas week and they were in the locker room at Capwell bus garage on the south side of the city. Having handed in their takings and dockets through the hatch to the accounts clerk, the drivers were preparing for home. On the wall was a large wooden rack with rows of named pigeonholes, where a bunch of keys or an envelope could be left for a colleague. As they chatted, my father reached over and removed three envelopes from the box with 'CP Creedon' on the front.

The conversation continued as he opened the first of the envelopes. Inside was a Christmas card from a Mrs Barry, saying how grateful she was to my father 'for keeping an eye on young Denis during the year when he was travelling to school on your bus'. There was a pound note inside the card. The second envelope had a ten-shilling note enclosed and the message wished him and his 'fine big family the best of everything in the New Year'. The third envelope contained a large card and another pound note. This was from an 'M. Heffernan' in Blackrock and read, 'Many thanks for stopping between the bus stops for me all year. I hope I didn't get you fired! Happy Christmas and God bless you, Mr Creedon.'

'Aren't people wonderful?' noted my dad. 'All we are doing is our job and yet they still go to all this trouble and expense for us.' He tucked the money and cards into his inside pocket and bade them farewell. 'All the best, lads. Have a great old Christmas now, let ye. Good luck!'

'I tell ya, that fella is some charmer,' said one of the other drivers. 'I mean, we all do our job the best we can, but you don't see passengers sending us money in the post. I tell ya, Connie Pa is some beauty.'

My father waited until March before announcing to his colleagues that he had actually sent those three Christmas cards to himself.

While the lads were still trying to make sense of this revelation, he delivered the killer blow. 'Of course, you do all know that envy is one of the seven deadly sins, don't you?' Game, set and match to Connie Pa yet again. He was a master of the practical joke. He wouldn't think twice about sending an anonymous letter to his son-in-law as a prank or a sheet of sandpaper, complete with stamp, as a postcard to a grandchild. You couldn't help but love him.

Poker or pranks, my old man knew how to play the long game. His hunches were good too. Many years ago he tipped Mick Mortell, a student in one of our bedsits, to become President of UCC (which he did), and our good friend Johnny Buckley, a student priest, to become Bishop of Cork and Ross (which he did). Then in 1993, a few years before he died, my father and I met the then Lord Mayor of Cork, Micheál Martin, at a function in City Hall. Micheál was with his dad, Paddy 'Champ' Martin, who was great old friends with my dad when they worked together at CIÉ. Dad took the opportunity to tell Champ that his son would someday become taoiseach. We all laughed our heads off when, in fact, we should have gone straight to the bookies – President of UCC, Bishop of Cork and Ross, and Taoiseach of Ireland would have been some treble. The lot of us could have gone off to Honolulu for the rest of our lives.

Still, a life on the road would always trump easy street for Connie Pa. He loved the people and stories that flowed through his day. It was all one big adventure. I remember being with him in the Westbury Hotel in Dublin a few months before he died. We were meeting up with my sister Marie-Thérèse and her family. At one stage I volunteered to accompany him to the 'tinny shed'. As we were passing through the lobby, a young waitress stopped in her tracks to let him pass. He acknowledged her kindness with a wink and his usual 'Good man, Julia'. She smiled back at him.

'You're an awful man,' I chided.

'Yerra, God help us,' he tutted. 'There's no harm in me and I s'pose I haven't too long to go now anyway.'

'Are you sure now this time?' I teased. 'You've been telling me that you're about to die for the last 40 years.'

'Well, I am this time, and I'm ready to go too. No problem. There's only one thing I'm worried about.'

'And what's that?' I enquired.

'I'm only worried that I might miss myself when I'm gone.'

I knew exactly what he meant. Although ready for the next life, he loved this life too. For all of the responsibilities that went with raising 12 children, Dad travelled light. It was life's unfolding story rather than 'things' that interested him. He often reminded me that 'there's no pocket in a shroud'. For Connie Pa, it was all about the journey.

On the night he died, I did the maths. He was driving a Model TT Ford from the age of 15, then he moved on to buses for CIÉ, trucks for the road freight and back to driving buses again until he retired on his sixty-fifth birthday. Limerick was 120 miles return, a round trip to Dublin was 320 miles, even Ballybunion was 200 miles return, and the spin to my mother's home in Adrigole was 140 miles there and back.

So, in his 50 years on the road, using the Cork–Limerick route as an average, he was driving 600 miles a week, giving an annual mileage of 31,200 miles. That would total 1,560,000 miles in his 50-year driving career.

Earth to the moon is 238,855 miles, or 477,710 miles return. In other words, my dad drove to the moon and back 3.2 times in his professional life. Add another couple of hundred thousand miles on the clock for a lifetime of private motoring with the family and we can conservatively estimate that he made four round trips to the moon from the day he was born to the day he died.

We know he crash-landed in Inchigeelagh in 1919, but I trust my man on the moon had a soft landing on his final return.

Gentle as the Fawn

She was modest as the cooing dove and gentle as the fawn
That roam over Desmond's storied heights,
those highlands o'er Gougane
No goddess fair in Grecian days in beauty could surpass
My winsome rogue, my Máirín Óg, my Inchigeelagh Lass.

– Excerpt from 'My Inchigeela Lass', thought to be written by Seán Ó Tuathaigh and composed by Jim Cooney

Both of my parents were born into an Ireland still ruled by Britain. My mother was two years younger than my father. She was born on 1 October 1921, a full 14 months before the 26 counties became the Irish Free State and almost three decades before they became the Republic of Ireland.

Life is never simple and neither are parents. My father was a talker; my mother was a listener. They loved each other dearly. While both my parents bemoaned the fact that the island of Ireland had been divided, they had no dislike of England. They listened to the BBC World Service on our big old radiogram in the kitchen and loved to see the Irish do well in Blighty. Singer Val Doonican and female impersonator Danny La Rue were huge stars in Britain and a source of great pride at home.

The musical repertoire in our car was led by my dad and included show songs such as Paul Robeson's 'Ol' Man River' alongside popular songs in the Irish language, *sean-nós* and light opera. Ballads of the 1916 Rising like 'The Tri-Coloured Ribbon' and 'The Foggy Dew' sat side by side with 'The Laughing Policeman' and classics from Gilbert and Sullivan's *HMS Pinafore*. The carload of Creedons would be in stitches at Dad's hilarious rendition of 'Barnacle Bill the Sailor' from the English music-hall tradition, where my father performed both parts: the big bass-baritone voice of Barnacle Bill the sailor and the falsetto of the fair young maiden. Whenever my father sang a verse from 'My Inchigeela Lass', especially the part about the cooing dove and the gentle fawn, I always felt like he was addressing my mother. He would have passed through that stunning landscape around Gougane on his way from Inchigeelagh back to visit my mother's home when they were courting.

Only once ever do I remember my father persuading my mother to sing. We were travelling west to Beara in the car and were taking it in turns to contribute to the sing-song. Rosaleen and Marie-Thérèse harmonised beautifully as they sang 'Frère Jacques', which they learned in school from the Ursuline nuns at St Angela's. Eugenia and myself belted out our usual party piece, the bawdy Dublin street ballad 'The German Clockwinder'. Eventually, after much persuading from my dad and loads of pleading from us, Mam agreed to try a song. She virtually whispered a beautifully shy performance of 'Bantry Bay'. When she ran out of words and said, 'That's all I have of it,' my father declared, 'This is not a sing-song any longer, children. What we are now witnessing is a recital! Well done, Siobhán!' We all cheered for her.

At various stages my mother was known by Hannah Maria Blake, which was her birth name; Joan, which some of her older friends called her; and Siobhán, as she called herself. I always called her Mammy.

Well, not always. Once I secured the right to roam, aged about six, I took to calling her Mam, an abbreviation favoured by the rest of the gang. I mean, you can't be threatening all-out war on the Dominick Street gang and still be calling your mother 'Mammy'.

My mother was the seventh sister of 10 girls born to William and Kate Blake of Crooha, Adrigole, on the stunningly beautiful Beara Peninsula. Beara, like its people, is both lush and durable. Like a finger pointing defiantly at the Atlantic Ocean, it faces the prevailing weather from the south-west and absorbs more sunshine and showers than most.

My mother loved her home place and spoke with great tenderness of her parents and the games of dress-up and make-believe she shared with her nine sisters. Although high on a hill, the Blake farmstead was protected from the bitterness of the north wind by the peninsula's ridge behind it. Their lofty aspect afforded them expansive views southwards across Bantry Bay and westwards along the peaks and valleys that ripple all the way to the ocean. Unlike the clamorous city streets of my childhood, my mother's memories of home were painted in a blur of watercolour brush strokes. Lush hedgerows of emerald fern with clusters of lemon-coloured primrose at its feet; swathes of saffron-orange montbretia and blobs of blood-red wild roses entwined in the burgundy fuchsia that went on for ever. Everything seemed so gentle: the neighbours, the collie, the cattle.

But underneath Beara's flourishing surface lay a harsh bedrock – reality. Bad land, big families and British rule led to incredible hardship and the inevitability of emigration. My great-grandfather Edmund Blake was born to John and Margaret Blake on 1 April 1844 and would have been just a baby, taking his first steps, as the shadow of famine crept up Hungry Hill. My grandfather, William Blake, was born in 1883. Unlike his namesake, the English poet, our grandfather knew real hardship. The post-famine years saw a trail of tears pouring down Beara's slopes and away to America. Somehow, William maintained his grip on the rock. However, all but two of his children were to leave Adrigole. In 1930, when my mother was aged 8, her older sisters Maura and Elizabeth, both aged 17, sailed for America. Maura eventually became a nurse and Betty went her own way, returning to Ireland just once when I was about 10.

My mother loved the pastoral poems of Padraic Colum, such as 'A Cradle Song' and 'An Old Woman of the Roads'. As a young girl, she read and reread *Ulrick the Ready*, a historical novel set in Ireland during the 1600s. It was written by Beara's literary giant Standish O'Grady.

She was softly spoken and subtle in her ways. For me, her outstanding characteristics included an artistic nature and a compelling need to nurture. Life with my father in the city afforded her the opportunity to blossom. She brought her considerable energy to healthcare, nutrition, education, art and antiques. She loved the political and philosophical debates that went on into the early hours with the steady stream of priests, professionals, musicians, artists and university students who passed through our kitchen to the music sessions upstairs in the sitting room.

She filled our bedrooms with encyclopaedias, classic novels, *National Geographic*s and huge bundles of *Look and Learn* magazines. Nothing was spared when it came to her children's education. At some stage or other, most of us would have been enrolled in the Crawford College of Art, Cork School of Music, Irish-language summer schools, swimming clubs and fee-paying schools until the money ran out. Don, my older brother, was a gifted musician and played a set of uilleann pipes that my parents had made by Leo Rowsome, the legendary pipe-maker.

My mother enrolled us in anything that might improve us. When I was no more than nine years of age, she sent me off on my own to see world-renowned violinist and conductor Yehudi Menuhin perform at Cork City Hall. All I remember of the event is sitting in a sea of blue rinses, surrounded by the ladies of the Cork Orchestral Society. I wasn't gone on the music but I liked all the attention.

ooo

The tailor Buckley, co-star of Eric Cross's book *The Tailor and Ansty*, had many solid theories. Once, when asked how he could know so much having travelled so little, he suggested that if you stood long enough at your own garden gate, eventually the whole world would come to you.

In Cork, the world came to my mother.

Although a shy woman, she loved the procession of characters who came to her shop counter. In 1941, a portrait painter named Johan Walland, who was serving on a Lithuanian freighter, jumped ship and wandered the streets of Cork City until the ship sailed without him. He found his way into our shop and my father commissioned him to paint my mother's portrait. He did and, despite her blushes, Dad placed that stunning oil on canvas over the piano in our sitting room.

On another occasion, in the late 1960s, a group of Russian sailors were in port for just one day. It was at the height of the Cold War and the Russians were keen to use the opportunity to buy some contraband from the West. However, it was a Sunday so the banks were closed, the sailors only had roubles and they didn't speak English. They eventually wandered down Devonshire Street, where our shop sign said 'Open'. My mother called us out to meet them, and after much hand-shaking and nodding and pointing and smiling, they left the shop with cartons of Wrigley's chewing gum, Pretty Polly tights and shampoo. They reciprocated with cartons of Russian cigarettes and two pint bottles of vodka. When I say 'pint bottles', that's exactly what they were – clear vodka with flip caps that you prised off with an opener. An interesting transaction for a woman who didn't drink or smoke; she just loved the novelty of it all. The contraband remained in the rarely opened drinks press by the stairs for a decade or more. Eventually, curiosity got the better of me and I borrowed the cigarette lighter and bottle opener from the kitchen drawer.

If Mam had any hobby, it was collecting. She wasn't a hoarder, just a collector. She catalogued emerging Ireland through her extensive collection of first-day-of-issue stamps, complete with postmarks. She also collected photographs, or 'snaps', as we called them. At a time when a lot of homes in Ireland didn't have a camera, my mother took photos of neighbours in wedding dresses and Holy Communion outfits, and we were allowed to borrow her camera going to football matches in case an opportunity arose to snap a celebrity. I was constantly being sent to the chemist with another roll of film for developing. In addition, she collected newspaper clippings on medicine, nutrition and world affairs, which she swapped by post with her eldest sister, Maura, in New York.

Otherwise, Mam rarely left the house when I was growing up. She was running a household of more than 20 people, as well as managing a shop that was open 19 hours a day, seven days a week. Furthermore, she took upon herself the well-being of relatives, neighbours and customers.

As a keen nutritionist, she would regularly waive the difference in price to ensure that less well-off children had wholemeal brown bread rather than the cheaper white sliced pan, which had become all the rage. The children of old neighbours from Beara would be sure of a place to stay and something to eat if they were in Cork for an exam or visiting a relative in hospital. She would constantly allow people behind the shop counter to use the phone in our kitchen, and she would make the call if the person didn't know how. In some cases, if the call was to a civil servant or a medic, my mother might actually represent the caller. After years of agonising, she eventually decided to get a coin-operated phone, hoping it would remind users, as she hadn't the heart to, that phone calls cost money.

At a time when my parents were struggling with a bank overdraft, my mother continued to pick up the tab for others. My father turned a blind eye. He never crossed my mother and the only time I remember him being cross with me was when I disobeyed her or gave her cheek.

One night, when a drunk who had been injured fighting on the street stumbled in the shop door, she refused to let the Gardaí arrest him. Instead, while a Garda held him, she dressed the cut on his forehead as he roared threats and obscenities at her. I had never before been in my mother's company when foul language like this was used. I blushed and her cheeks flushed.

When the Gardaí had released him on his bond to 'go straight home', I asked her why she had nursed a man who was cursing her. Embarrassed by the scene we had both just witnessed, she looked away and headed back towards the kitchen. Over her shoulder, she softly replied, 'Yerra, to err is human and to forgive is divine. He was some poor woman's baby once.' My immediate comeback was ... silence, as the fundamental truth of what she had just said landed.

It didn't mean that I wouldn't get the silent treatment myself for some misdemeanour, but the truth of what she said that night has stayed with me. Forgiveness comes easy to me.

Mam also had a wonderfully wild artistic streak; I just wished she hadn't expressed so much of it through me. Once, when a parcel from America arrived containing a pair of second-hand lederhosen, the kind of leather shorts worn in Bavaria, she uttered the words I came to fear: 'These will fit John.' My 'I'm not too sure, Mam, none of the other boys wear leather shorts' fell on deaf ears as she convinced me they were grand. Secure in the reassurance of a woman who loved me, I sashayed out the front door of the shop, only to retreat moments later to a chorus of teenage neighbours shouting 'Hitler!' and 'Ye little Nazi!'

It was the same when slip-on shoes with elasticated panels were invented. A godsend for a mother of 12 on a school morning, hell for the only boy in a class of 51 who didn't have shoelaces. Then there was my mother's choice of Confirmation name for me.

'Roncalli,' says she.

'Ron who?' says I.

That's exactly what the Christian Brother said too: 'Ron who? Roncalli? That's Pope John's family name. You want to be called John Roncalli like the Pope, is it?'

Whack!

Although I paid the price for my mother's flamboyance on a few occasions, I loved her dearly and yearned for her approval. Praise was not something she distributed liberally. In keeping with the times, many Irish parents erred on the wrong side of giving a child a big head, or 'elephantiasis of the cranium', as my father loved to call it.

I can only remember one occasion when I had Mam and Dad all to myself. They were probably aged around the 50 mark and we were travelling to Dungarvan to visit my mother's sister Eileen. I entertained them from the back seat with a selection of Republican ballads that I'd learned in school. As we descended the slopes to Dungarvan, I noticed my dad stretch his left arm across the back of the passenger seat and rest his hand on Mam's shoulder. In a soft tenor voice, he wooed her with song fragments:

Darling, I am growing old,
Silver threads among the gold ...
But, my darling, you will be
Always young and fair to me.

The three of us savoured the moment together as the car hummed away eastwards. My dad knew she was the most beautiful woman in the world, and that's kind of the way I felt about her too.

Sex on the Wall

The smell from Patrick's Bridge is wicked
How does Father Mathew stick it?
Here's up 'em all,
Says the boys of Fair Hill.

– Excerpt from local song, possibly penned
by Seán O'Callaghan of Blackpool, Cork City

By a mere bowl-hop, I can call myself a Norrie. We are the one hundred thousand or so souls who live along the spine of Cork City, that hard, bony ridge of red sandstone that runs from Sunday's Well on the western edge of the city to Glanmire at the other. Cork's Northside tumbles down the hills like rivulets to the Lee; Strawberry Hill, Buxton Hill, Richmond Hill, Patrick's Hill, York Hill and Summerhill all lead to the bridges and quays of our neighbourhood. Hannie Mac, who lived at the top of Fairhill, claimed all the steep hills had put a hump on her back from years of dragging the shopping back up home through the Northside.

Our neighbourhood, like most city centres, didn't have a name. The suburbs had names and all the other areas of the city had names – Mayfield,

Bishopstown, Ballyphehane, Douglas – but we didn't. Similarly, our patch didn't have any clearly defined boundaries. Most kids know where their territory begins and ends, but our turf was a loose blob of city centre, where the neighbours and the borders kept on changing.

We liked to think it was a tough neighbourhood. Someone even wrote the word 'sex' in chalk on the gable-end wall of Tommy Connell's house once. One of the Kenny boys told me it was to frighten nuns and other people. He warned me to say 'nothin' to no one'.

Someone else drew what looked like a huge letter 'W' on a wall on Pine Street. I had already started my schooling, so I recognised it as a capital 'W', but Donie Collins told me it was a drawing of a woman's boobs. I wasn't in the better of it.

Today, the old neighbourhood is home to tapas bars, lap-dancing clubs, a comedy club, a couple of theatres, a number of casinos, a bowling alley, amusement arcades, pool halls, hotels, Asian supermarkets, halal food suppliers, a Russian bar, a Polish shop, Chinese restaurants, Japanese restaurants, a mosque, several pubs and a wet house run by Cork Simon Community. This palace of variety runs from Leitrim Street along Devonshire Street to the top of MacCurtain Street – a strip of little more than 200 metres.

Sixty years ago, when it measured a few hundred yards and I was strutting my five-year-old stuff, it was equally exotic, but in a more polite way. O'Brien's Café sold home-made ice cream from under its Chantilly-style candy-striped canopy, where students from several of the nearby secondary schools dawdled and played with the straws in their ice-cream floats. In the shop window of HCC office supplies next door, toy soldiers staged lavish battle scenes. Just across the street, Hadji Bey's sold home-made Turkish delight and chocolate.

Like the Inchigeelagh Dairy, many of the shops bore the names of the family's origins, like the Iveleary Bar, which had its roots in my father's parish of Uíbh Laoghaire. The fishmonger's across the street proudly disclosed its source on the sign over the door: 'Baltimore Stores'. I recall its thick bevelled-glass shop window that ended about an inch shy of the downward-sloping windowsill. Ice-cold water constantly flowed across the window display of fresh fish, with their grotesque faces and thick lips. The water would then follow the chiselled groove and disappear down the drain. The expression of the huge monkfish that served as an eye-catching centrepiece of the display reminded me of one of the nuns in St Angela's. All of the other fish were wide-eyed and looked like they must have died with their eyes open from the shock of it. In contrast, the pigs' heads in the timber barrel outside O'Sullivan's shop had their eyes and mouths closed and looked far more resigned to their fate. I wondered what expression I might have on me when I died.

The Munster Hotel was home to the Hilton nightclub and hosted showbands like Eileen Reid & the Cadets, the Clipper Carlton, Art Supple & the Victors, and Ireland's top cabaret stars, like Hal Roach and Joe Cuddy. The male stars all smoked, wore cufflinks and smelt of aftershave. The women wore miniskirts with plastic knee-high boots and walked with their arms folded.

Just up the street were the Twelfth Night and Monty's, nightclubs which provided a welcome space for Cork's considerable gay community, and the Metropole Jazz Club ran till late. At the same time, down the street, I was standing on a chair behind the counter of a shop that only closed its doors when the last of the stragglers had gone home.

Our neighbour Rory Gallagher plied his trade and paid off his Fender Stratocaster by playing with the Fontana Showband, all the while hanging out with beatniks, hippies and rockers at the Cavern and the Cavalier Club on our street. It was in these clubs that my brother Don and my sister Geraldine drank coffee with bearded guys called Len De La Cour and Joacim Boske.

Don could make the uilleann pipes soar and, accompanying himself on guitar or mandolin, he would deliver the songs of the great American protest singers of the time: Dylan, Guthrie, Seeger and Paxton. Geraldine, beautiful in a minidress and a necklace she had made from melon pips, sang Joan Baez and Buffy Sainte-Marie. And together they would harmonise with the Sun Folk, their group.

I collected pop pictures. Margaret O'Sullivan, who worked in our shop, would always bring me back the publicity pictures that were handed out by showbands at dancehalls. I would reciprocate her kindness every time I got back from a chat with the girls who worked in McCullough Pigott on Patrick Street. They were probably in their thirties and forties, while I was only aged seven or eight, but I always got a great welcome when I ambled across Patrick's Bridge and in the door with my standard 'How're the girls? Any new pop pictures?' They'd let me in behind the mahogany counter to rummage through the new records and they'd give me shiny black-and-white showband publicity pictures. I'd always ask for extra ones for Margaret.

However, behind the city's bohemian veneer lay pockets of real poverty. Sometimes, particularly when I travel in the poorest countries of the southern hemisphere, I'm reminded of how dirty many of the streets of my own time and place really were. The children of the shanty towns who point at my big white knees and run away giggling are oblivious to the greasy smell of rotting household waste, white dog shit and eye-stinging wood smoke in which they live. It mirrors back to me the greasy smell of rotting household waste, white dog shit and eye-stinging coal smoke that went unnoticed in many of the laneways of my own childhood.

We giggled at tourists too, although apart from a passing bus on its way to Blarney or Killarney, we saw few holidaymakers. Cork City had to wait another 30 years to become a buzzing city-break destination. But I do remember seeing a coachload of elderly Yanks climbing out of a CIÉ tour bus outside the Metropole Hotel on MacCurtain Street one day, and two of them were wearing Levi's. Paudie Leary thought it was hilarious.

'I'm not jokin' ya, two of 'em, as ould as our parents and they both wearin' jeans! And that's not the half of it,' he laughed. 'One of 'em was a woman. I swear. A big old-woman's arse up on her and she baked into a pair of jeans, like mutton dressed as lamb. They're gone now. But Creedon seen them too, didn't ya, Creedon?'

'I did, shaggin' ridiculous,' I confirmed.

At this remove, I suppose the tourists must have looked to us a bit like me waddling around Zanzibar in a pair of shorts. Shaggin' ridiculous.

ooo

Cork City began as Corcaigh Mór Mumhan (the Big Marsh of Munster). In the seventh century, St Fin Barre established a monastic settlement amongst the Celtic tribes who lived there. Wave after wave sailed up the harbour: Viking, Huguenot, Jew, colonist and refugee. As the swamp was drained to create quays and malls and bridges, Patrick Street emerged from the horseshoe shape of the river that preceded it, and nearby Drawbridge Street tells its own story.

Our neighbourhood on the north bank of the swamp was established as a busy trading hub by Danish Vikings in AD 900. A stone inscribed 'St John's Mill 1020 AD' was discovered on nearby John Street in 1920, suggesting that the Kiln River, which flows in from Blackpool to join the Lee, was already harnessed to turn the watermills of breweries, tanneries and the multitude of little tinpot industries that gave the immediate area its nickname, 'Little Baghdad'. It appears as 'Greene Marsh' in 1759 and later as 'Devonshire's Marsh', named after the Quaker family who bought it.

Soon after, two Antrim brothers, John and Isaac Carroll, also Quakers, inherited the area. They developed a huge timber business there in the 1770s, building Carroll's Bridge across the Kiln and providing us with the street names and playgrounds of our childhood. Carroll's Quay, where we fished for eel, Pine Street, where we kicked a ball and played street games like 'All-A-Bah' and 'One, two, three, the book is read!' Carroll's Sweet Shop on the corner was the source of penny bars, lucky bags and caramels at four for a penny. When Betty Carroll died and her shop became an African food store, the centuries-old connection with the Carrolls, the Quakers from Antrim, faded. Gone in the ebb and flow of life in a port town.

I grew up on Devonshire Street West. But our next-door neighbours, O'Connor Bros. Undertakers, were actually on Coburg Street and the people across the road lived on Leitrim Street. Suffice to say, the neighbourhood was a confusion of place-names, many of them commemorating British military might. We had Wellington Road, Hardwick Street, Trafalgar Hill, Grosvenor Place, Wellesley Place, Belgrave Place, and the continuation of our street was once known as King Street – but we got that one back.

On 20 March 1920, the city was traumatised when Lord Mayor Tomás Mac Curtain was assassinated in front of his family. The shooting took place on his thirty-sixth birthday at his home, just out the road from us at Watercourse Road in Blackpool. Within a month, the incoming Lord Mayor of Cork,

Terence MacSwiney, proposed a motion to change the name of King Street to MacCurtain Street in honour of his predecessor. A Sinn Féin majority in City Hall ensured the motion was carried.

By 25 October of that year, Mac Swiney himself had died in Brixton Prison following a 74-day hunger strike. Soon after came independence for the 26 counties. The names of the 1916 leaders were then commemorated in street names all over the city. The main railway station on nearby Glanmire Road was renamed to honour Thomas Kent, a Corkman who was executed in 1916. Victoria Barracks, up the hill from our house, had been named to mark the visit of Queen Victoria to the city in 1849. However, by 1922, the British Army was lowering their flag and handing Victoria Barracks over to the Irish Free State Army, who renamed it Collins Barracks after their first Commander-in-Chief, Michael Collins, another Corkman.

ooo

City centres are rarely designed with children in mind. There were certainly no playgrounds or football pitches where I grew up. Schools had concrete yards, but playgrounds existed only in English comics, as far as I knew. Fitzgerald's Park on the Mardyke had a slide and some swings and roundabouts, but it was half an hour away. You could kick a ball around Bell's

Field at the top of Richmond Hill all right, but the slope was so steep that if your ball ran away down Patrick's Hill or Richmond Hill or the Fever Hospital steps, it became someone else's ball. We just improvised on the tarmac and concrete fields of the city centre.

None of us went to the same school and not everybody knew where everybody else lived. We were just a load of kids from the city centre who congregated and played football endlessly.

There was Henry Condon from Emmet Place, who lived in the British Legion Club where his parents were caretakers; Dónal Sweeney, one of the only people I know who actually lived on Patrick Street, because his parents had a flat on the top floor of Woodford Bourne's Grocer's & Wine Importers. There was Bollicky, a fella who lived near the Mardyke and was always knocking around. Then there was Spud Murphy, from Fairhill, one of the youngest, who collected dirty words. Hundreds of them. He taught us everything we needed to know.

'What's a hure, Spud?'

'A man with a leg and a half,' Spud replied.

'Really?'

'Yeah,' says Spud, 'Granda Carr was shot in the war and lost half a leg. My dad always says he's a harmless ould hure.'

Once we were chased out of a school yard by a religious Brother. From a safe distance Spud shouted back at him, 'G'wan, ya shaggin' lesbian, ya!'

'What?' said Henry Condon.

'They're all lesbians in there.'

'Naw, they're not lesbians. My mam says they're Redemptorists.'

'Same thing!'

There wasn't a house with a garden anywhere near us, so any ball that was booted over a wall became wedged on the roof of a warehouse and we had no way to retrieve it. We would say, 'Ya ghoul, you banished de ball.'

On one such occasion, we decided to call up to Bollicky and get a ball off him. We knew where his house was 'cause we often waited outside for him to come out. His mam was one of the mothers who would never let any kids into their house, so we had no idea what was in there, except our noses told us that she was constantly boiling bacon and cabbage.

Up on tippy-toes, I picked up the door knocker, which was shaped like a wrist and fist, and gave it our usual one-two, one-two, one.

As I waited for a reply, I wondered who might come down the hall to answer the door. *Either his mam or his dad, I'd say, 'cause his sister is very small.* As I prepared my greeting, suddenly the awful reality struck me: 'Jesus, lads! What's Bollicky's real name?'

Sweeney and Condon shrugged and looked at each other as if expecting that the other might know the answer. They both shook their heads and Sweeney said, 'Naw, no idea. Never even thought about it.'

At that very moment, the door opened and his dad greeted me with a blunt 'What?'

I had no choice. I had to go for it.

'Eh, em ... is, eh ... is Bollicky in?' I chanced.

He looked me up and down before he spoke.

'I'll get him now for ya,' he replied, turning on his heels and half-pushing out the door.

ooo

Any bit of wasteland or derelict site became our playground. We once got a whole summer out of an abandoned Morris Oxford car in Knapp's Square. We'd meet up there after tea and go for spins to Youghal or America. I wanted to bring seven or eight of us to London once, but no one wanted to go and Small Timmy started crying 'cause his big brother was a Dagenham Yank who got knocked down and killed by a train in London. So I told him I was sorry for saying 'London' and we drove to Manchester instead to see Georgie Best. He was grand again then. I can still remember the smell of damp stuffing from those car seats as I practised going through the gears without the benefit of a clutch, because my feet didn't reach the pedals.

You could also have a right good adventure helping the older lads push-start a stalled car. Car owners were constantly looking for a push in those days and I got the starring role once. Donie Murphy from Home Farm Stores had gone to the rescue of a Ford Consul that had conked out at the top of Coburg Street.

'C'mon, lads, fall in there,' he instructed. 'Put the small lad in, he'll be lighter.'

I hopped in and Donie adjusted the seat. 'Are you all right there, kid? Leave it in second now and keep your foot on the clutch until I give the shout.'

'OK.'

'That's right now, stand down on it good and hard. Don't touch the choke or you'll flood her. D'ye hear me now? We have only one go at this while we have the fall of ground.'

'OK.'

'Drop the handbrake on the first shout ...'

'Right.'

'... and foot off the clutch on the second shout ...'

'OK.'

'... then stab the clutch to the floor again if she starts or you'll tear the hole out of the gearbox.'

'Grand.'

'But hey!'

'What?'

'There won't be a third shout 'cause you won't hear me, you'll be motoring.'

'OK.'

'And remember, when she starts, keep your foot on the clutch and hit the footbrake or you'll go flaking into Betty Carroll's window. Just keep her revvin' till we catch up with you.'

'Grand.'

The biggest fear for the pushers was that their exertions might actually work and the car would take off suddenly, leaving them with their chins hopping off the tarmac.

'All right, lads, on a count of one ... two ... three ... Heave!'

Away we went, the scrum and me. Four burly lads at the boot, slackers at the side and my size four on the clutch.

'Right! Now ... Now!'

'What?'

'Now, for fuck's sake. NOW!'

I whipped my foot off the clutch – the car lurched, coughed and started purring like a kitten. We had ignition. I looked down and hit the brake pedal in the middle, exactly as I was told, and then started revving the accelerator pedal over on the right like mad. However, nobody had reminded me about looking out the windscreen and steering the vehicle, while I was looking down to find the pedals. The car mounted the pavement with a bump and came to a sudden stop at Corcoran's bins. It didn't matter. No one was hurt and I kept her lit by vroom-vrooming until Donie Murphy caught up with me.

Unfortunately, I was to get too good at starting cars.

Often the back of an untended lorry would become the deck of our pirate ship as we repelled boarders at any price to them or us. Four or five of us would establish dominion over the truck and face down hordes of screaming smallies. The youngest were too tiny to climb, so they just ran around waving home-made flags and shouting, 'Death to the pirates!' Like extras in a Tarzan film, smallies were expendable. Families were big so there was no shortage of them, and another wave would be along in a moment.

However, bigger kids were well able to clamber up the sides and over the tailgate or side rails of a truck. As soon as a head peered over the rim of the truck, it would be shoved to the ground below, complete with the body that was attached to it. At the first sign of a hand reaching over the side, a pair of rubber dollies was brought down on the fingers with a grunt: 'Ahar, me hearties!'

But as we learned in school, *an té nach bhfuil láidir ní foláir dó a bheith glic* (the person who isn't strong had better be clever), so even a smallie will eventually find a way to fight back. An unexpected assault would be launched at the least vulnerable part of the truck – the front. A couple of smallies would scamper over the bonnet and, holding the wipers to steady themselves, would get up onto the roof. This now gave them the high ground as well as the element of surprise. In fairness, you couldn't really fling a smallie off the roof of a lorry without their mother or, worse again, their big brother hearing about it.

On other days we would sneak into McKenzie's Mill to watch the men watching the hoppers as tons of seed poured down the wooden chute to be crushed into animal feed. The pour would begin like the sound of hailstones on a shed. The entire cascade would land in a heap, puffing a rolling cloud of dust and husks into the air. Powerful men like Dan Mescall would stand there, hands on hips, motionless, until the pour had landed. It was a welcome moment of meditation before the men snapped out of their reverie and resumed the rhythm of their work.

The warehouses along Pine Street were stacked to the roof with canvas bags full of seed. 'Get off the bags!' was the well-worn cry of the men as they sensed us clambering over the towering mounds of bags. They were worried we might fall down a crevice between the bags and be suffocated; we were scared they would lock us in the warehouse overnight or, even worse, tell our mams. They never did either, even though they spent half their working day shouting, 'Come down off those bags!'

Apart from McKenzie's, there were loads of other workplaces that operated an open-door policy for curious kids. Ned Ring's forge, behind the brewery, was a haven of banging and clanging, with white-hot irons and giant brown horses. Paddy Daly, a cabinet-maker on Lower John Street, had a huge back yard. Apart from shouting an occasional 'Keep away from the electric saws!' he turned a blind eye to the dozens of boys and girls flaking each other with timber blocks and sawdust.

Tadgh, an elderly man, worked in a loft on John Street preparing coffins. We would often call in to him on the way home from school. I loved the sweet smell of varnish and fresh wood, and I marvelled at the speed with which he could screw on the brass handles.

One day, while leaning into the coffin to staple the snow-white lining over the straw padding, he delivered his usual wisecrack. 'They're all dying to have a go in one of these.'

'Can I have a go?' I asked him.

'Stapling? Oh God, no, you're too small yet. You'd make a bags of it.'

'No, I mean, can I have a go of the coffin?'

'You want to get in?'

'Yeah, it looks cosy, but don't put the lid on it. Promise?'

'G'wan so, but kick off your shoes first and be quick about it.'

I climbed in, then I folded my arms across my chest, closed my eyes and sucked in my cheeks to look dead. Tadgh and all my pals roared laughing. In fairness, Tadgh never even threatened to put on the lid. Just as well – I'd have died!

Outside on the street, bags of rubbish were routinely dumped in open spaces. Most people chucked a few bags over Carroll's Quay wall from time to time, into the river and gone with the tide before daybreak. The Lee delta was one big self-flushing cesspit in Viking times. Even in our times, bags of rubbish and human excrement would happily float along both channels of the River Lee, as dockers inside the early houses along the quays could be heard singing the praises of 'the green leafy shade on the banks of my own lovely Lee'. Deep down, everyone knew that rivers were for fly fishing, not fly-tipping, but it took another generation or two for it to stop.

Apart from the rubbish, flotillas of white swans would sail up and down the Lee. Once, when conditions were stormy, I counted 60 swans sheltering and preening themselves on the concrete slopes of the Kiln River.

Our freedom of the city's streets didn't come without risk. I got a belt of a car on a few occasions, and there was always some kid on the missing list from school. At roll call, the missing boy's name would be answered with a chorus of 'He fell off the top of a factory wall, sir' or 'He got his head split wide open by a belt of a rocker, sir.' Like notches on a stick, scars were great scorekeepers. I once gouged a considerable chunk out of my calf muscle while heaving a plastic fertiliser bag of rubbish out of the way of our favourite goalpost gate. I failed to notice the sheet of broken glass sticking out of a slit in the plastic. And every time Tony Tobin got a haircut, he would show us where he got the back of his head split wide open by a hurley.

But there were greater dangers. At times, the Kiln ran red with blood from the slaughterhouses upstream. Other times it ran porter brown. The rats were huge from gorging themselves on eggs and chicks from the hatchery, animal ration from the millers and everything the homes and small factories of Little Baghdad regurgitated into that stream like there was no tomorrow. And for some there wasn't. One of our neighbours drowned while playing on the steps inside the quay wall. Other children got sick.

In 1956, Cork experienced a terrible polio epidemic. There were twenty deaths nationally, with five fatalities in Cork, and numerous survivors were left with disabilities. I wouldn't be born for another two years, but words such as 'callipers', 'iron lung' and 'fever hospital' became part of everyday conversations. Dr J.C. Saunders, the city's Medical Officer of Health, ordered the closure of the outdoor public baths at the Lee Fields and issued warnings through the *Examiner* and the *Echo* that swimming in any part of the Lee was to be avoided, as the entire city's drainage flowed into the river. People were discouraged from travelling into or out of areas of the city where the disease was prevalent, and parents were encouraged to put their children to bed before nightfall.

The warnings came too late for my brother Don and for several other children on the street. They carried the pain of polio for life, and so did many of the parents.

ooo

Like much of Ireland, Cork has weathered more than its fair share of hardship, but its people are resilient and love to talk. 'It's good to talk' is something we're constantly told nowadays, but we already knew that and, like most people who live in teeming inner cities, we were good at it.

The farmers who tied up their donkeys and carts outside McKenzie's were quiet, though. Their words were few and far between, and I also came to love the quiet spaciousness of my boyhood summers in the countryside.

I still feel most at home amongst the chatterboxes of the less well-off neighbourhoods of the world. I grew up in an age when few families had a car, so children just walked everywhere. Walking and talking, that's how we made sense of the world.

For better or worse, bus journeys used to be a shared experience, before earphones became the norm. Queues were for talking to strangers and the sight of an eight-year-old boy and an elderly lady at a bus stop chatting about Jack Lynch was par for the course.

Our shop provided a stage where an endless cast of characters created the soundtrack to our childhood. The streets seemed full of smallies and shawlies, and every one of them was a storyteller.

Blessed Martin

Hannie Mac, from the top of Fairhill, collected holy memorabilia in the same way that Spud Murphy collected bad words. They were both well known for their wealth of knowledge. When Hannie wasn't talking to any person in particular, she could be heard mumbling the Litany of the Saints to herself: 'Lord, protect us. Saint Paul, pray for us. Saint Thaddeus, pray for us. Saint Barnabas, pray for us ...' The clutch bag under her shawl was like a tabernacle of saints. Inside were blessed palm from Knock, rosary beads from Lourdes, a thread from Padre Pio's mitten, holy water from Fatima in a plastic Virgin Mary bottle and a relic of the True Cross given to her by a priest just back from the Missions.

Whatever about the relic of the True Cross, her friends implored her to put the priceless thread from Padre Pio's mitten into a vault in the Munster & Leinster Bank on Bridge Street. She wouldn't hear of it. 'No way, gurl. Anyone trying to rob that from me will have to kill me first and then they'll go to hell on a double-mortaller.'

I presumed she meant a double death sentence for murder and for attempting to steal a sacred object. We thought a sentence of life in the electric chair would do the trick nicely. Hannie herself, of course, would go straight up to heaven, just like everyone else who managed to die for their faith. Martyrdom was as perfect an end-of-life outcome as any of us could ever hope for, as long as it was relatively quick, not like poor ole Blessed Oliver Plunkett, who was hanged, drawn and quartered. When a boy in school with an incessant curiosity for dates and history asked Brother Finnegan 'When exactly did Oliver Plunkett die?', Brother Finnegan lost his patience and roared, 'When they chopped his bloody head off!'

God knows, Hannie did her share of suffering too, and not only did God know, but all of Cork knew as well. She told us all, regularly. She was demented from worry, crippled with arthritis, and every night, instead of sleeping, she died a thousand deaths from heartburn. My father referred to her list of ailments as 'The Litany of the Complaints'.

Hannie was also heart-scalded from her husband Jerry's laziness. Not only had he failed to hold down any kind of job, but he was even struck off the dole for not getting up in the morning to sign on. The man in the labour exchange told Jerry he was 'un-unemployable' and stopped his payments.

On 28 June 1963, Hannie came into our shop, complaining about her husband to my mother. 'He wouldn't get up to see John F. Kennedy, Mrs Creedon. The whole Northside was above in MacCurtain Street all morning waiting for the President of

America to show up and my fella was above in bed waiting for his slice of toast.'

Back then, before television and mobile phones, any old distraction would draw a crowd. If someone dropped a bottle of milk on the street, they'd be instantly surrounded by what the *Cork Examiner* used to describe as 'curious onlookers'. If a submarine or a liner or some unusual boat docked in the harbour, the word would get out and the multitudes would descend on the quays. Nothing actually happened. The men just stood there in dark overcoats with their hands in their pockets or smoking fags. If a house caught fire or a car broke down or there was a funeral, they'd be there again, standing and looking.

Like most martyrs, Hannie blamed herself. ''Tis me own fault, gurl. I'm too good to him. But y'know yourself, when I sees him hungover above in de bed, I don't have the heart to call him.'

Jerry was mild-mannered, but possibly the laziest man I have ever met. A neighbour once claimed that Jerry's idea of chivalry was to hold the door open for Hannie when she was going out to the yard to get a bucket of coal for the fire. The misery seemed to suit Hannie, though, because she knew it would secure her place in heaven.

Her favourite saint was Blessed Martin de Porres, a handsome Dominican brother of mixed African and native Peruvian ancestry. He died in Lima, on the same date that I was born: he died on 3 November 1639 and I was born on 3 November 1958. I took this as a sign that I was destined for something great, maybe even martyrdom.

While Blessed Martin was revered in our local Dominican church, strictly speaking, he wasn't a saint. But you wouldn't want to argue that one with Hannie. As his title suggested, Martin was merely 'Blessed' at the time, but he was on his way to canonisation and it would be a great day for the Northside if and when he got over the line.

Like many of the boys on my street, I wanted to die for Ireland, preferably in a church while shooting from behind the altar as we made our last stand against the Brits. This would be followed by a state funeral. I'd be laid out in the North Cathedral, with a bloodstained bandage around my head to hold my brain in place. Everyone in Cork would queue for hours to file past my coffin, some of them hoping to rob a thread from my uniform and others picking up an extra blessing by touching my mother's shoulder and whispering, 'I'm sorry, Mrs Creedon. You can be rightly proud of him ... he died for Ireland. You have to be strong now.'

Hannie would undoubtedly be at the top of the queue of old ladies, blubbering over my open coffin so she could discreetly dip her hanky in my wounds and secure a priceless relic for her collection.

Most houses at the time displayed symbols of faith. Many would have a holy water font at the front door and a Sacred Heart picture with a little red light flickering beneath it on the kitchen wall. Some years before I was born, our house caught fire, part of the kitchen ceiling collapsed and that very picture fell off the wall. When the firemen retrieved it from the smouldering rubble of the kitchen, it was perfect. It had fallen face first from the wall and, despite the intense heat and flames, it was intact, apart from a few large paint blisters on the frame. My father re-painted it gold, but decided not to sand the blisters away so they would serve as a reminder to us all.

ooo

The old radiogram in the kitchen hummed away from dawn till dusk, through meals and homework and all. On school mornings the kitchen was full of chatter until Andy O'Mahony was about to come on the wireless with the news. At that point my father would say, 'Will ye whist up and hiren it.'

My sisters took turns at the breakfast table, serving in the shop and minding 'Baby John'. They brushed my hair, fed me soldiers of warm buttery toast and made me laugh. What more could a little boy ask for? God, I loved them all so much. Still do.

The girls would form an orderly line of plait-weavers, as the older ones ensured the smallies made the standard expected by the Ursuline nuns of St Angela's. Then, as suddenly as it began, the cacophony of Creedons was gone in a flurry of green uniforms, blazers, berets and gaberdine coats. A trail of girls' voices faded out the shop door, leaving my mother and me with a few hours' peace and quiet to ourselves.

My mother was in and out of the shop to attend to deliveries, as Miss Healy, our shop assistant for 20 years, stacked the shelves. I was sitting on my little chair, and a two-pin plug at the wall socket trailed tantalisingly before my eyes. I examined my box of crayons and pencils to find one that would fit so I could twiddle my pretend screwdriver in the hole like a fixer-man. A Blessed Martin pencil, complete with picture of our hero from Peru, was the perfect size.

I pushed the pointed pencil into the hole and put the other end between my lips to light my pretend cigarette. Lead in a pencil is a conductor of electricity, but fortunately the wooden body of the pencil and the rubber eraser at the top act as insulators. However, the tin surrounding the eraser to hold it in place is a conductor, so ... pufftt! I went up in smoke. My mother turned to see why the electricity in the house had tripped and she shrieked like a banshee when she saw a wan and lifeless ragdoll flopped on the chair where her bouncing baby boy had been sitting a moment earlier.

I don't remember much after the flash. As I came round three or four days later, the light hurting my eyes, I tried to piece together what had happened and why my two hands were bandaged and covered with snow-white cotton mittens.

I soon found out that the best part about being sick is the attention, and the worst part is the boredom. In the pre-screen era, I erased the hours by drifting in and out of sleep. A lullaby leaked in through the badly fitted sash windows. It was the distant sound of the men in McKenzie's yard shouting instructions to each other. 'Back her in there, Tom. Hould it! Hould it! Dan, drop down the hoist ... mind the bags. Haul away, Charlie ...' I was gone to where little boys go, dreaming of being a big worker-man.

Whenever I was awake, the blue flowers on the wallpaper provided a distraction. I cracked the code. Every six flowers down, the pattern repeated itself. The big bunch with five flowers ran over the border onto the next roll. My dad must have known how to make them join up because you wouldn't notice the joins unless you were sick and bed-ridden.

At night, I would wake in the dark not knowing what time it was. I could see my mother's bedside clock, but I didn't know how to read the time. I could count, however, so I'd lie there until the Shandon bells chimed the time to me.

A cobweb dangled from the bedroom ceiling and swayed if someone opened the stairs door. Any time the cobweb stirred, I cocked an ear, listening and wishing for the creak on the third step on the stairs that heralded a tray with beef-tea and toast and maybe a comic from the shop window. No creak on the stairs meant it was only Mother Cat going about her business, probably padding her way to her perch on the south-facing windowsill at the turn on the stairs. From there she could warm herself while watching the row of overfed pigeons perched along the rusty drainpipe on O'Farrell's roof, which covered the warehouses full of grain seed and animal feed on Pine Street.

She was some survivor. As a kitten, she had twice been rolled over by a car. The second time the vet said her hips were broken and she would be unlikely to have a family. He got that bit wrong. She had a number of families, but we had them all adopted. My mother hadn't the heart to have her spayed, as the poor craythur had already endured her share of surgeries. So any time a litter of kittens was due, the ad went straight into the *Evening Echo* and up on the shop-door window: 'Beautiful tortoiseshell kittens. Free to a good home. Phone Cork 20913.' Any enquiry was met with 'They're not here just yet, but they should be ready for collection in about eight to ten weeks. Can I take your number and we will call you then?' I expect the caller hung up convinced that we were either making kittens to order or had the gift of prophecy to describe them as 'beautiful tortoiseshell' when they had yet to be born. But invariably they were beautiful and tortoiseshell, and great fun too.

○○○

When I had recovered and life went back to normal, the one-on-one special attention stopped. Mam had a range of other lesser crises to deal with now. I was beginning to feel disappointed that I hadn't woken up dead in the North Cathedral and that the bandages weren't on my head. That would show 'em. My opportunity for martyrdom had been snatched from me by the bloody do-gooders in A&E at the Infirmary.

Mind you, they had the decency to leave me with a few serious wounds where the electricity had earthed. There was a hole the size of a half-crown on my right wrist and another the size of a sixpence at the top of my left thumb, which had left me with no thumbprint. This was a serious loss, as the Brits could now nail me on my fingerprints alone.

However, once I was well enough to parade my wounds around Devonshire Street, I realised that I had, in fact, attained hero status: 'Dere's de Creedon boy what fused the whole Northside.' At every invitation to 'show us de wounds', I would happily adopt my martyr face, slip down a mitten and peel back the generous layer of waxy yellow penicillin gauze to reveal an oozing open wound.

'Jeeesus!' Mrs Daly would say. 'Look at de state a' dat!'

She and Hannie Mac put the icing on the cake for me when they announced that I was the subject of a miracle cure.

'Oh yeah, sure a nurse above in the North Infirmary said de poor child took an awful jolt of electric altogether. Sure, he blew thousands of bulbs all over Cork. He'd have died if he hadn't used the holy pencil. If it wasn't for Blessed Martin he'd have been ashes. Blessed Martin is the man. No doubt about it. Even Brother Dominic says it. A miracle.'

The subject of a miracle cure? This was music to my ears. Sure that's only one step away from being a saint.

When Spud Murphy called down after tea, I told him. 'Hannie Mac said that what happened to me is a miracle.'

'Wha'?'

'She said Blessed Martin saved my life.'

Spud raised one eyebrow. 'He wha'?' he asked incredulously. 'Blessed Martin saved ya? He did in his hole. He nearly killed ya!'

Maybe, but we thought it best to say nothing to anyone and let Blessed Martin keep the credit lest we ruin his chances of getting over the line.

Sure enough, a few months later, Pope John XXIII canonised him in Rome. I'd like to think I played some small part in that result.

Family Pass

For decades, Córas Iompair Éireann, or CIÉ, as most of us referred to it, was the umbrella company for virtually all public transport in the state: buses, trains and haulage. My dad began working as a bus driver in Cork City in the late 1930s, switching to driving trucks with the National Road Freight during the Emergency. He hauled mostly livestock and lorryloads of turf from the bogs of rural Ireland to the Phoenix Park, where it was stacked into two huge banks on either side of the Avenue, which became known to Dubliners as 'The New Bog Road'.

Britain's war effort required increased productivity from its collieries, so they didn't feel any obligation to supply to a neutral country like Ireland. By order of the newly appointed Minister for Supplies, Seán Lemass, turf was harvested at record pace. Thousands of men migrated to the midlands of Ireland to cut more than half a million tons of turf by hand for the fireplaces of Dublin. Most rural folk already had access to a local supply of turf, but gas was rationed in Dublin, so turf became the only way to keep the home fires burning.

I remember my dad telling us of an eating house in the midlands where he and other drivers would stop for dinner when hauling turf cross-country. Dinner was in the middle of the day and the menu never varied. It was bacon on Monday, bacon on Tuesday, bacon on Wednesday, bacon on Thursday, fish on Friday, bacon on Saturday and bacon on Sunday (if it was open). The host, a tough old woman, was filthy from feeding pigs, stoking the turf fire and the lack of running water.

'Yerra, the filth was cat malojen all right,' said Dad. 'I mean, she had a face full of huge blackheads and you could sow a drill of spuds under her thick fingernails. Someone christened her Snow White and the Seven Warts and the name stuck. Ah, she was deadly, I tell you. She'd wipe her nose on her apron, or on the tablecloth if it was closer, but by Christ you wouldn't cross her!'

My father's gift of acceptance was admirable and stood to him in times of war and want.

He claimed it would be no surprise to come in and find the tomcat asleep on the table or a hen grumbling to herself as she picked her way between the diners' legs, pecking at the droppings from the table amongst her own. A big old sow, oblivious to the menu, would often come sniffing and snorting around the back-kitchen door to see what was on offer. The pig would be dispatched, squealing, with a boot between the cheeks of its backside by the hostess with a 'Clear off, you smarmy bitch!'

As inconvenient as a world war can be, it was a poor excuse for the state of her kitchen. Any request for a little gravy or white sauce to lift the game would be instantly dismissed, as if entertaining any variation of the menu were a sign of weakness. 'Yerra, g'way back up to Dublin for yourself if 'tisn't good enough for you,' she'd say. 'White sauce is right. Isn't hunger the best sauce of all?'

She had a point. But the tedium was cruel.

In an effort to break the monotony of the menu and the tyranny of Snow White's refusal to concede ground, a driver named Byrne from Dublin procured a jar of Colman's mustard.

A volcano of bursting spuds tumbled down onto the newspaper in the middle of the table. Snow White delivered a plate of steaming hot bacon and sopping wet cabbage. Rather than risk the wrath of the chef, Byrne waited for herself to clear the kitchen, and only then dipped his knife into the jar of mustard, dropping a nice big blob onto the side of his plate.

Before he could make his next move, Snow White was back, brandishing another dinner. Her beady eye spotted the foreign object on Byrne's plate. She lifted the corner of her apron with her free hand and, without breaking her stride, swept the yellow blob from Byrne's plate with a sigh. 'Bad cess to 'em. Them friggin' hens, they get everywhere!'

My father often spoke of the responsibility of travelling solo through the night and of trying to change a huge and heavy back wheel with a load of cattle aboard. This was a real test of self-sufficiency and the reliability of the jack that came with the Leyland. As the Emergency receded, he was relieved to get back to life with a conductor and two-legged customers and do what he did best – talk.

As an employee of CIÉ, my father was entitled to a reduced rate on CIÉ trains, plus an annual family pass. Although a drain on CIÉ's resources, this was a godsend to a family of 14. Every year, without fail, my father would present himself at the station master's office at Kent railway station to collect the pass. He'd walk along the sweeping curve of its polished platform, his footsteps echoing from the glazed red bricks, until he came to the mahogany door with STATION MASTER printed in an arc on the frosted glass. Dad would tap on the glass and wait.

Eventually, when it was good and ready, a voice with a pronounced North Cork accent and a deep sonorous tone groaned, 'Come in.'

That would be him, the station master.

As soon as my father's head came round the door, the station master, without greeting him, would lift the receiver of the heavy black Bakelite phone on his desk, sigh and, without dialling any number, would *olagón* into the phone. 'Hello? Is that the goods yard?'

Pause.

'Right. Put another carriage on the Dublin train. The Creedons are going to the a-zoo.'

Once the gag had been delivered, he'd raise an eye to my father and ask, 'Well, Connie, what was it this year?'

'Another boy, Jim.'

He'd stoically write out the family pass and in the same droll fashion say, 'Enjoy Dublin now, let ye. And bring us back a shtick of rock.'

And that was that, until the same time next year.

ooo

Travel was rock 'n' roll back then. Buses, trains, planes and the ferry to Britain – they all rocked and they all rolled. People got sick on buses, trains, planes and especially on the ferry to Wales. A huge number of people would have described themselves as 'nervous travellers'. Hannie Mac claimed she would never go abroad: 'I gets all the sun I need goin' in and out the backyard to the line.'

Hannie's view was eventually vindicated when we got the horrific news that our good friend Maura Herlihy from Betty Carroll's sweet shop on Pine Street corner was listed among the 61 dead in the Tuskar Rock air disaster of 24 March 1968. Aer Lingus Flight 712 had crashed into the sea. We all loved Maura and I still remember the right kick she got out of me, and the broad smile on her big face, the day I innocently asked her, 'How much are the penny bars, Maura?'

A grey cloud descended on the street when the news landed. We were all kept off the street for a day or two, but Maura's dad and her sister Betty rarely cast their shadows on the street thereafter, and the family's long association with Carroll's Quay and the old neighbourhood soon ended.

In the days before unbroken rails and silent carriages, train travel had some particularly attractive rhythms. The traditional broken rail produced the clickety-clack beat that infused a thousand blues songs. Announcements over the carriage speaker about 'Portlaoise, Portarlington, Thurles and Ballybrophy' had a musicality, as well as a train tempo. And if you stood on the rubber mat that covered the join between the carriages, you could look down at the blur of sleepers and hard-core beneath your feet.

If you got permission to take your baby brother to the jacks, you could use the opportunity to stick your head out the window, despite dire warnings about the priest who was looking back along the track, counting the number of carriages coming on behind, and never saw the bridge coming on in front as it smashed his skull. They say his head was found miles away.

This was a time when the configuration of a standard train carriage was conducive to the oul' chat. Two double seats faced each other with a common table to share. Conversation was a common courtesy.

'Are ye all going to Dublin?'

'We are. Up to see our cousins in the zoo! And yerselves?'

'I'm afraid not. This poor maneen beside me is going up for a little operation.'

'Is that a fact? I'd say you'll be right as rain before you know it. Will you have a sweet? Good man.'

In the old days, when we were small and our parents had money, we'd all troop up to the dining car like the von Trapp family. It was expensive, but the breakfast in the buffet car was the Orient Express of Irish travel in the 1960s. The waiter wore a uniform like they did on ocean-going liners. A piping-hot breakfast plate with two sausages, two rashers, two pieces of pudding, a grilled tomato garnished with parsley and a perfectly basted soft-fried egg. A selection of brown bread and toast was accompanied by little scrolls of butter and two tiny pots of jam and marmalade. Tea was served in a teapot with the CIÉ logo, and a little gold line ran around the inside of the teacup. This 'high tide mark' served as a reminder not to overfill the cup lest the train's motion cause the contents to splash and scald.

Once in Dublin, we'd troop out of Heuston Station, or Kingsbridge, as my parents always called it. My mother would sometimes slip away into town to do a little discreet Christmas shopping in Hector Grey's toy shop on Mary Street. My father would shepherd his flock up to Dublin Zoo. I loved the monkey enclosure and always wondered if they thought we all looked the same. Maybe Marie-Thérèse and myself did.

The return journey to Cork always seemed interminable, but once we reached Mallow we were on the home stretch and everyone knew it. Once the train lurched out of the station, the excitement would heighten. Like lions at feeding time, passengers got restless and some even started pacing.

By the time the red-brick chimney stack of the Sunbeam Wolsey woollen mills in Blackpool came into sight, the entire carriage was on its feet, stretching to reach the baggage rack, tidying up tables or spitting on handkerchiefs and wiping children's smigs. They say the Cork crowd get homesick even when they are at home. That's exactly how it felt as the train disappeared into the 'mile tunnel'. In the darkness, impatient passengers gathered around the carriage door. There would be a loud screech of metal on metal as the brakes were applied and the iron wheels ground against the rails. Someone whispered, 'Jeeesus! We'll all be kilt!' But of course we weren't. Instead, we were reborn – delivered out of the tunnel and into the loving arms of Cork.

Rite of Passage

My father he works in the sewage,
He works there by day and by night,
And when he comes home in the evening,
He's covered all over in ...
Shine up your buttons with Brasso, shine up your buttons with Vim,
Shine up your buttons with Brasso, it's only three ha'pence a tin.

– Excerpt from an old street rhyme,
'Shine up Your Buttons with Brasso', anonymous

'Shine up Your Buttons with Brasso' was just one of a latrine-full of bawdy ballads bequeathed by the British Army to the children who lived in the lanes around the barracks near our house. Although they continued to provide much of the soundtrack to street games for generations of inner-city kids, our parents would have 'mombolised' us if we had been heard singing them.

For years, I thought that song was actually about my dad. Although a bus driver by profession, my father did spend more than his fair share of time in the sewage. You see, the sewer system in our house was a couple of centuries old and, in fairness, it had served its purpose as best it could. But as the household went from single occupancy in my grand-aunt Julia's time to double occupancy when my dad came to join her in 1931, then to the purchase of the house next door, the extension at the back and the rapidly increasing number of people under its roof, the plumbing was literally creaking and leaking at the seams.

By the time I was press-ganged into holding the sewer rods and my nose as Dad plumbed the depths to clear yet another blockage, the household had grown to over 20 people, with two bathrooms and, in the event of emergency, the old reliable – the tinny shed.

Depending on wind and tidal conditions, my father and myself could be around the side of the house with the manhole cover open, screwing one sewer rod into the next and inserting the plunger up whatever pipe my father thought was the most likely culprit.

'Pass me down the claw.' The 'claw' was a sewer rod with a brass corkscrew attachment at the top that replaced the plunger head, which ensured the operator now had a grabbing head to pull out any blockage. Three or four vigorous plunges followed by a quick withdrawal and ... gurgle, gurgle, whoosh!

'Christ! Hairballs! If I've told them once, I've told them a thousand times. WOULD. YE. PLEASE.

For the LOVE of God ALMIGHTY and his Blessed MOTHER ... STOPPP flushing ye'er hair down the conswilly?!'

Then he looked at me. 'And Jesus, you're nearly as bad as 'em!'

'Me?'

'Yes, you! Whatever about your sisters and their own hair-brushing and plaits and all the rest of it, they have you turned into a girl too with that ole mop-top. They're making a sissy out of you and an eejit out of me.'

'Yeah, but,' I argued, 'there's a picture of you up on the piano, the one of you in Inchigeelagh when you were small, and your mam had you in long hair and a girl's dress.'

'Yerra, that was only a petticoat, so the fairies wouldn't steal me. They didn't steal girls. But there's no fairies now and you only look like an oul' sissy. We'll go down to Moriarty's barbers and 'twill only take ten minutes. You'll be just like me.'

Just like you? I thought, as I glanced at his thinning white thatch with the bald patch in the middle.

'But Seanie Carr has long hair,' I protested.

'I know he has, and sure that's fine. If Seanie Carr wore a bikini, would you wear a bikini? Would you?'

I probably would, but I knew the right answer was 'Eh ... no.'

'I've nothing against long hair, it's just that it doesn't suit you. Good man, we'll go down now once we have the rods put away. It'll make a man of you.'

I didn't want to be a man. I was only six. But a small boy is no match for the bluster of a parent intent on steering him into 'what's best for you'.

He dropped the metal lid on the sewer with an unmerciful crash and, while he kept up a non-stop litany of assurances and inducements, we hosed the sewer rods clean and stacked them back into the old canvas sack under our stairs. Within the hour I was climbing the barber's stairs to meet my fate.

ooo

Moriarty's barbershop was upstairs over the Lee Garage on Merchant's Quay, then a wonderfully one-sided, higgledy-piggledy parade of architectural varieties. There was the Art Deco bus station, or the 'Bus Office', as we called it. Dad worked there. Then came the faded Victorian grandeur of Queen's Hotel. There were a number of little shopfronts with small-paned Victorian bay windows, exactly as they were in 1858 when Charles Dickens made his way to Cork Opera House for three public performances. He packed the place and read from his newly published book, *A Christmas Carol*, before travelling to Blarney to kiss the Blarney Stone in the hope of acquiring the same gift with words as his Cork audiences. Wickham's was still there with oil lamps in the bay window when I passed a century after Dickens. Then came Crowley's Music Shop, where Rory Gallagher bought his first guitar and I bought rosin on my way to violin classes at Cork School of Music. Ironically, the men's hostel, a modernist block with frosted windows, sat amongst several pubs, including the Pig & Whistle with steps up to the front door, before you came to Kilgrew's toy shop, where children would crowd against the glass, hypnotised by window displays and aching for Santy to get it right this year. Moriarty's barbershop had a panoramic view across the broad north channel of the River Lee and away over the slopes of Cork's Northside, laid out like a dining table. Shandon provided the pepper pot, and the big square tower of the North Cathedral was the salt cellar.

Using a series of mirrors, Mr Moriarty had every angle covered. If someone came up the stairs they were lamped, even though he was facing the opposite direction. With his hand-held mirror, old men could examine their own bald patches once a month.

Although the shop was a man zone, bad language was not tolerated. A glance in the rear-view with a raised eyebrow was enough to silence even one of the Teddy boys who lived up by the barracks. A stack of well-thumbed old copies of the *Evening Echo* and

Daily Mirror with missing racing pages sat on an empty Brylcreem box, ready to be passed down along the queue to anyone tired of waiting. Sometimes fellas would share a fag and talk about dogs and pigeons and hurling.

A faded, cream-coloured price list was pinned beside a bird cage with a chirping canary. The sign read, 'Gent's haircut 2/6. Boy's haircut 1/6. No credit.'

On Saturdays, the queue would stretch out to the four kitchen chairs on the landing and continue down the stairs. Without looking up from their shoelaces, self-conscious young men would volunteer their chairs to older men, while invisibly maintaining their places in the queue. Eventually, Mick Moriarty would flap the previous customer's hair cuttings from the cape and shout, 'Who's up?' over his shoulder.

My father, *plámás*ing me, said, 'Look, I have to go to work. Just stay in the queue there, here's two bob. Give it to Mr Moriarty and tell him to let the bone be his guide. He'll take his one and six out of it and you can buy sweets on the way home with the change. Don't get lost on me now, will you? Your mother would go mad.'

With a nod in the mirror to attract the barber's attention, my father again mouthed the instruction, 'Let the bone be your guide.' He then winked a quick 'Will you be OK?' in my direction. I shrugged a 'Sure' and he was gone.

My friend Dónal Sweeney told me that barbers had a razor and they would slash your throat if you spoke.

Like the conveyor belt of life, the sudden stop at the end is unavoidable, so sure enough the cape was flapped and Mr Moriarty barked, 'Who's up?' while eyeballing me.

I shyly crossed the floor and, using the footrest as a step, I climbed onto the big swivel chair with all its pedals and levers. Mr Moriarty had a short length of timber that he placed across the armrests so little boys came up to barber height. This little boy felt like a king as Mr Moriarty placed the cape across my shoulders. Using the pedal, I was elevated to a position whereby I could survey the entire city laid out before me.

Mr Moriarty spoke nicely to me and said the same things that every adult said to me when they heard my name was Creedon. 'Your father is a gas man. Did he ever tell you about the day the man died on the bus? Or did you hear about the day he won a live harbour seal in a raffle below in Crosshaven? He brought the seal up to Cork in a barrel in the back of the bus and we released him into the harbour just below the Bus Office.'

It felt like everyone in Cork knew someone in my family. Old men would regularly say, 'Jesus, your mother was the most beautiful woman in Cork. We used to cross town just to have a look at her.' Younger men were always asking things like, 'What's your sister's name? Y'know the dark one like Liz Taylor?'

'Yeah, that's Constance.'

'Is that your sister, the blonde nurse?'

'Yeah, that's Carol Ann.'

'She's a fine half.'

'I know. Everyone says that about them all.'

I settled into the sound of the men's conversations, enjoying the low buzzing of the electric clippers and soothed by its fizzy sensation on my neck. Mr Moriarty would have you tilt your head forward to ensure you had clean lines all round. I rested my chin on my chest and peeped upwards at the bottle of Bay Rum used for scalp massage and the Mac's Smile razors on the shelf. The wrapper on the blades had a brilliantly comic drawing of a frowning bald man with stubble on his chin. If you turned the blade wrapper upside down, he was smiling with a smooth chin and a crew cut on top. Miraculous!

To finish, Mr Moriarty prepared his own barber's razor – the 'cut-throat razor'. He stropped the blade on a leather strop, whipped up a head of shaving foam and slopped it expertly onto the back of my neck with a soft pig-bristle shaving brush. *Here it comes*, I thought, as I flexed my shoulders and braced myself for the first feel of cold steel on my skin.

It was brilliant. Didn't hurt one bit and afterwards my neck felt as soft as my baby brother's face. *This is like being a man. My first shave. I could be a soldier or a cowboy or anything I want now.*

∘∘∘

Walking home along Merchant's Quay, across Patrick's Bridge and up Bridge Street, I began to wonder if any of the mams with the shopping bags thought I was handsome.

I decided to take off my sports coat and, with the index finger of my left hand through the loop inside the collar, I swung it over my shoulder, like the dockers did on a hot day. I started to walk like the Teddy boys and whistle like the men did when they were coming out of the pubs on Coburg Street.

My right hand was jingling the change in my pocket and I thought, *No small thruppenny bar of Cadbury's chocolate for me no more. I'm getting chewing gum, like the Teddy boys. The spearmint golfball ones.*

As I sauntered around Falvey's corner onto Coburg Street with my hands in my pockets and chewing gum like a murderer, I spotted Dónal Sweeney and Henry Condon on their hands and knees on the footpath outside the Greyhound Bar.

'Hey, Sweeney, are ye playin' marbles?'

'Naw,' he barked, 'there's a shaggin' ten-bob note down there in the areas.' He pointed down through the metal pavement grille used by breweries to access the cellar where the beer barrels were stored. Dropping to my knees, I squinted incredulously. 'Where?'

'Down there ... look!'

And sure enough, 10 feet below street level, lying delicately atop a mound of sweet wrappers, crisp bags, fag butts, empty Sweet Afton packets and dirt, there it was ... a bright-red ten-shilling note.

'If we go into the bar and say we dropped it, they won't believe us, and the men will just get it and drink it themselves. Henry's goin' to go home to get his old man's fishin' rod to see if we can hook it, but if he's caught takin' it he'll be murdered.'

'It's a ten-bob note, not a fish,' says I. 'Like, it's not goin' to bite the hook. It'll only keep movin', ya langer. We'll be tryin' that till we're spotted by the men in the pub.'

Whatever about the ten-shilling note, the penny also dropped, eventually.

'I have it!' I announced. 'Come on, hurry down to our house and watch the shop in case my mam spots us,' I ordered.

I slipped in through the shop and, without stopping, I smiled to acknowledge my mother's compliments about the haircut. I kept going before she came up with something for me to do and grabbed the canvas sack of sewer rods from under the back stairs. The boys were waiting out of sight of our shop window as I came out the side door. We walked back up the street in giant strides rather than draw attention to ourselves by actually running. As we went, I selected the rod with the claw and removed it from the bag, smiling like an innocent.

'Will you be able to grab it with that?' puffed Henry.

'Naw, this claw's comin' off,' I announced.

Removing the brass claw, I gave my mouthful of spearmint gum one last chew before I sacrificed it for a higher purpose. I stuck the gum to the brass tip of the rod and, assuming my father's role as boss of the sewer rods, I instructed Sweeney to pass me another one. 'C'mon, be lively about it.'

Henry was ordered to adopt the marbles posture as a decoy for our covert activity.

Gripping the rod firmly in my fist lest I drop it, I lowered it through the grill, and as Sweeney hastily added three more rods, down went the gum tip into Aladdin's Cave. Once it was in position, Sweeney whispered, 'Now!' In one stabbing move, I harpooned the prize.

'Bull's eye!' said Sweeney, trying to maintain his restraint.

Next came the delicate process of withdrawing the rods without losing the prize. I continued as director of operations. 'Just put a finger in on either side of the bars, and when I get it up to the bars, keep the ten bob pressed up against the gum. Careful, willya!'

And just like that, we became the richest kids in Cork. The Milky Bars were on me, but clearly we weren't going to try cashing the money with my mother in our shop, so it was straight down to Betty Carroll's shop on the corner of Pine Street. 'Three big bars of Cadbury's, please, and six spearmint golf balls.'

Outside, stuffing our faces, Sweeney finally acknowledged the obvious. 'Where did you get the bazzer? You're like one of the Teddy boys up by the barracks.'

'Yeah, I know.' I dismissed him mid-chomp. 'Sure, I was only chattin' to them earlier when I was inside in Moriarty's for a shave.'

A Neighbour's Child

Seanie Carr was my next-door neighbour and I worshipped him. He lived in No. 3 Devonshire Street and was nine years older than me. He had a mop-top hairstyle and looked like Paul McCartney from the Beatles.

Seanie followed Man United, so I followed Man United. Seanie listened to Radio Luxembourg, so he taught me how to find it on the wireless in our house and I listened to Radio Luxembourg too. He let me play darts on the dartboard that hung on the inside of Carrs' hall door. He even brought me to the Wimpy on a date with his girlfriend once. I spotted them holding hands and kissing, so I went out to the jacks.

I was a regular in Seanie's house from the time I could walk. I'd just wobble to the next door down, their front door, and it was always open.

When I learned to run, aged about two or three, I'd call to Carrs' house on my way back from posting cutlery in the post box on the corner of Pine Street and Camden Quay. When you're number 10 of 12 children, living in a busy shop, it's simple to slip out the door when the phone rings or another sibling is crying. If you can run, you've got the head start on the sister in pursuit. So, as long as I was out of earshot of the alarm call – 'Quick, Baby John is gone with the cutlery again' – I'd make it all the way to the post box and get the stuff in the opening. The gift of cutlery was on its way to Santy now and there was nothing my sister could do about it, except say, 'I'm telling Mammy you wouldn't come back, even though you definitely heard me.'

By the second time I had successfully made the run, the postman had been tipped off and knew exactly where the mystery objects rightly belonged, so he'd drop them in to my mam on his way past.

However, there was no retrieving my little shoes. When Eugenia told me that the swans in Carroll's Quay slept on the river at night, I was concerned they might be cold. So, at every opportunity, I would kick off my shoes and chuck them over the quay wall with the declaration 'Shoe shoe bon bon!'

Carrs' continued to be a safe haven until I outgrew it. If I ever needed refuelling, whether with bread and butter or self-belief, Carrs' was always a reliable pit stop. The household included Seanie, his father, Dick Carr, who was a retired train driver, his mother, Mrs Carr, and his grandfather, Granda Carr, who wore a hat, had a moustache and had lost a leg in the war. Out in the backyard was Rex, their black cocker spaniel. I think he was fed up with living in the yard because he was fierce cross altogether and I wasn't allowed out to use their tinny shed unless one of the Carrs was with me.

Seanie had an older sister, Norma, who was grown up and gone for most of my childhood. There were older brothers, too, but I never met them because they lived in England. I think they might have been Dagenham Yanks.

I can still see Dick Carr sitting inside their front room, leaning to one side in the armchair as he tried to manoeuvre the *Evening Echo* into the solitary shaft of daylight that limped through the sitting-room window. It wasn't much, as all the houses on our side of Devonshire Street faced north towards Richmond Hill – and the sun never came over that hill. Furthermore, Mrs Carr, like most of the mams, used a fine-filament net curtain and a geranium in a brass pot on the windowsill to keep things private. Sometimes Dick would move the brass flowerpot to one side of the sill to allow the daylight see the sports page. No sooner had he moved it than Mrs Carr would be back in with a tut to re-centre it.

'Come out of my light!' he'd say.

'Your light?' she'd say.

The plant and pot had been given to Mr and Mrs Carr as a wedding present 30 years earlier, so it was much older than Seanie.

You see, Seanie was a surprise baby and Mrs Carr loved him to bits. She loved me nearly as much.

I knew this because, although the Carrs weren't wealthy, Mrs Carr used to put tons of butter on my bread. She also allowed me to sit in Granda Carr's wheelchair when he was upstairs in bed. He didn't mind me using it either. In fact, when I was very small, I was allowed to squeeze in beside him in the wheelchair for the grub. I loved that old black war-veteran wheelchair with its levers and wheels. It was like having my own car.

Seanie had loads of friends his own age, but they were scattered all over the Northside. That's the thing about growing up in a city centre. Unlike housing estates, where all parents age together and children grow up in parallel, city streets are populated by old ladies, lonely old men in flats, students in bedsits, out-of-towners and a very light sprinkling of kids. So it wasn't unusual to find yourself hanging out with someone nine years younger or older than you. We'd take all sorts into our gang. There was an eight-year-old who lived over a pub with greyhounds in the yard, a fella from Belturbet, Co. Cavan, with an English accent who we simply called 'English', and the teenager whose dad was a surgeon in the Bons. It was a broad church. So there was nothing strange about Seanie and myself kicking a ball around Pine Street or strolling out to the Lee Fields on the far side of the city. Seanie was like a big brother to me and I was as handy as a small pot to him. If either of us was at a loose end, we'd simply call next door.

All of our neighbours were very close. We hadn't much choice in the matter, as Devonshire Street was a row of houses without front or back gardens. The window of the bunkroom where I slept overlooked the row of backyards all along the rear of Devonshire Street. You could clearly see into Carrs' at No. 3 as well as a good chunk of the whitewashed wall of the Lanes' house at No. 4. But as the angle decreased, so too did the view, until it was reduced to a glimpse of a cat on a tin roof at the O'Connells' house in No. 8.

Every house had a tinny shed in the yard. Dick made his daily trip to the outside jacks of No. 3 at around the same time every day. I could just about spot him from the window of the top bunk, his trousers down, one white knee keeping the jacks door slightly ajar to allow him enough light to read the *Echo*. Sometimes I'd make a farting noise out the window and duck before I was spotted. Once, when I was feeling really bold, I ran down to our yard, found a metal bolt and washer, lobbed it over the high wall and waited for it to land with a deafening 'KERRANG' on the galvanised roof of the Carrs' tinny shed, followed by Dick's bellowing in the wrong direction, 'Hoi! Get ooouuuutttt of it. I know that's you, Christy Lane!'

ooo

I loved when Seanie called into the shop and asked my mother if I could go to the cinema with him. If *I* asked her, she might say no, but she wouldn't refuse Seanie. I'll never forget the time he brought me to see the Beatles' *Help!* I was only six years of age, but I remember the hysteria in the Lee Cinema that afternoon as hundreds of teenagers released the frustration of trans-generational shame, modesty and restraint.

When I got back, Miss Healy and Margaret were on duty behind the shop counter, waiting for my report. They hung on my every word as I delivered my blow-by-blow account. Margaret said she'd faint if she ever met the Beatles, but Miss Healy said she'd have no interest in a man with a mop-top.

This was a time when hundreds of schoolboys armed with cap-guns and catapults would pack the cinemas for the matinee Westerns on Saturdays. Cries of 'Look out behind ya!' and 'Scalp him!' filled the air. Whenever a cowboy or an Indian was shot dead, the entire audience, on a count of 'One, two, three!', would shout in unison at George, the usher, 'Georg-ie! Take out de body!'

Fred Bridgeman, who worked at the Savoy, was one of Cork's biggest celebrities, but few would have recognised him in the street. You see, Fred only ever performed in the dark, with his back turned to his audience, so nobody ever saw his face. When the lights went down and the plum-coloured velvet curtain went up, Fred would emerge, astride his huge organ. Women would cheer, men would shout 'Dowtcha, Freddie boy!' and a full house would sing, 'Oh! I do like to be beside the seaside'. Two thousand faces, illuminated by the ever-changing hues of pink and jade and turquoise reflecting from the screen, would stare up at the moving dot as it bounced along the onscreen lyrics in time with the accompaniment from Fred's Compton organ. His audience sat there, ecstatic, necks craned as though witnessing an apparition by the Blessed Virgin herself. All of us from Cork, all of us together, and all of us basking in the reflected glow of showbiz.

In a time when Ireland's voiceless did what they were told, nothing was as tempting as roaring something back from the relative safety of the bleating flock. Posh people had the letters page of the *Cork Examiner* and the *Evening Echo* to voice their displeasure with something or other. Clearly, they didn't feel the same need to release their frustration by roaring in public ... but by Christ, we did! Cork people love shouting from a packed audience, and Seanie and I were no different.

Under the cover of darkness and surrounded by your own tribe, you could urge on the Apache with a burst of 'Scalp the bollox!' or 'Look out behind ya!' If any patron tried to quieten the offender with a 'Shush!', their attempt would be met with an even louder 'Shush!', followed by someone trying to outdo the previous 'Shush!' until the entire cinema was shushing and shishing and falling around the place laughing.

Nobby, the cinema commissionaire at the Palace, would be running around with his torch, threatening to stop the film. He was a former British Army sergeant and he got a job in the picture house because he looked the part and was happiest when in uniform. Some people said he got shell-shocked in the trenches. Well, if he did, it was a minor test of his nerves compared to the torture he endured every Saturday afternoon from pups like us.

Nobby's attempts to suppress the shushing would result in the poor man himself becoming the moving target as cries of 'Nobbyyy!' went up from different parts of the crowd. If he ran down the aisle with his torch to investigate someone up the front shouting 'Nobbyyyy!', someone in the back corner would distract him with 'Over here, Nobby boyyy!' As he turned and raced back up the red carpet, sweeping the back rows with his search light, a voice from the balcony would scream, 'Up here, Nobby, ya bollox!'

Invariably, the cavalry never came for Nobby. He had to deal with the savage natives on his own.

Eventually, two or three innocent patrons were headlocked and given the door.

Once, the entire Apache nation was chasing John Wayne across the silver screen. Most kids were shooting at the Apache, who were closing in on the lone cowboy. Eventually the Apache braves found their range and three arrows thudded right in the middle of John Wayne's back. Without missing a beat, Seanie shouted out, 'One hundred and eighty!' Even the kids who were shooting at the Indians fell around the place laughing.

Years later, my good friend Bernard Murphy told me that when the Palace eventually closed its doors, the workmen who took down the giant silver screen found hundreds of dead cowboys and Indians in behind it.

The Sound of One Hand Slapping

There's never a one of all your dead more bravely died in fray
Than he who marches to his fate in Toomebridge town today;
True to the last! True to the last, he treads the upwards way,
And young Roddy McCorley goes to die on the bridge of Toome today.

– Excerpt from 'Roddy McCorley' by Ethna Carbery

At the age of six, I made my First Holy Communion and moved on to the big boys' school with the Christian Brothers.

The following year, Ireland would mark the fiftieth anniversary of the Easter Rising. Every school in the state was to fly the Tricolour and every classroom was to display a framed copy of the 'Proclamation of the Republic'. Amongst its many fine aspirations, this noble document declared that all the children of the nation should be cherished equally. This part of the proclamation somehow seems to have been misunderstood in communications between the Irish Republican Brotherhood, who issued it, and the Irish Christian Brotherhood, who operated several schools in the city and two in our immediate neighbourhood.

Rather than cherishing all of the children of the area equally, the Christian Brothers had, in fact, streamed the boys into two lanes that ran parallel to one another up the Northside slopes: one for the fabulously rich and the other for the fabulously poor. Rarely the twain would meet.

The boys attending the fee-paying Christian Brothers College, which was up the hill to the right of our front door, played rugby, spoke English and mostly went on to careers in the professions or in business. The boys attending the non-fee-paying Christian Brothers North Monastery, which was up the hill to the left of our front door, played hurling, spoke Irish and mostly went on to work in factories, the civil service or the dole.

On my first day at primary school, I came out our front door and turned left, up the hill to the North Mon.

All told, it was a fairly sharp turn, given that the first few years of my life had been spent in the protective bosom of my mother and doting sisters. The next five years would be spent in a classroom with 50 other boys and a man with a leather strap.

I walked the 20 minutes up to Fairhill and joined the other 203 new boys in the yard. We were each assigned a class. There were four classrooms of 51 boys per class. At any one time, the North Mon Primary School had a thousand boys in attendance. At the end of the five-year cycle, most of the boys who hadn't already fallen off the conveyor belt simply crossed the sprawling campus to the North Mon's secondary and technical schools.

There were so many boys in the school at that time that when it came to our lunch break, or *lón*, as it was called, we had to march in single file around the schoolyard for our own safety. There was no way a handful of Christian Brothers could marshal a thousand screaming Norries.

Fifty-one boys to every class and I was the youngest, a pattern I maintained throughout my life. I was keen to try everything, even when I wasn't ready for it. But, as is often the case with big families, if you're good to go, you're gone. Next! I was the youngest kid at everything: school, Scouts and the Gaeltacht. My discharge papers from the FCA at the age of 18, following five years' honourable service, serve as evidence that I was wearing a uniform and carrying a gun at the age of 13.

The severity or otherwise of the school regime varied widely, depending on the temperament of the Christian Brother standing at the top of the class. My first teacher was the red-haired Brother Gill. He was both a gentleman and a gentle man. However, a whole range of personalities, and in some cases a few personality disorders, lay behind the uniform black soutane of others. The enforcer was also uniform – a standard-issue thick leather strap, known as *an leathar* or the leather. Had there been a weapon of choice, I expect some would have opted for the lion-tamer's whip and chair to control 50 wild boys in a room. I suspect many of the Christian Brothers had as much interest in being there as ourselves.

Our classes were through Irish, so I had a bit of catching up to do. My favourite subjects were *Gaeilge, Béarla agus Tír Eolas* (Irish, English and Geography), but I really struggled at arithmetic. I've since come to realise that if you don't understand addition and subtraction, you're unlikely to ever grasp multiplication and division, and try as I might I drifted further and further out to sea. I could count, though, and knew well what 'six of the best' meant.

If summoned to the top of the class, we knew it wasn't for a gold star. So every defensive measure was employed by the dead man walking. Shuffling slowly from the desk when summoned in the hope that the teacher might count to 10 himself. Smiling a goofy smile at him in the hope that he might think you looked too small and cute for a right lashing. Raising your arm and presenting your palm at as high an angle as you could to shorten the arc of the downward swing to reduce the impact was another attempt to lessen the blow, literally. No hope. His left hand would grip you around the wrist of your receiving hand and lower it to where the palm would be met by the lash at its most ferocious. In the shadow of the crucifix and the executed leaders of the 1916

Rising, we were encouraged to 'take it like a man'. We did our best. I hated getting slapped. I also hated it when anyone else got slapped or started crying.

Once back at your desk, you could cool your stinging palms by loosely gripping the cold cast-iron legs of the desk. If you were spotted, however, a few more 'reminders' were administered.

'Well (WHACK!) ... we'll just have to (SLAP!) ... warm up those little hands for you again (SLAP!) ... won't we (SLAP!)?'

The class would laugh at Teacher's little joke. It was better to humour him than not. You could always reveal your true feelings about him to your best friend, in my case Gerard Healy, on the way home. But you couldn't really tell your mam you were in trouble in school again, could you?

Gerard said the *leathar*s were made up the country by nuns. We also heard that they were made up the country by girls who were mams. Either way, we all agreed that someone who didn't know us or why we were getting slapped definitely shouldn't be packing *leathar*s into boxes and sending them around the country.

Brother Healion, a kindly man from Mayo, was school principal. He eventually decided that enough was enough and the leather was kept under wraps in his office, unless specifically requested by a teacher. A teacher would have to send for it if he wanted to use it. I expect Brother Healion felt the two-minute walk to the office would serve as a sort of 'timeout' during which the teeth-grinding, purple-headed rage of the celibate one might subside. However, in practice, it wasn't the teacher, but the victim, who made the slow walk along the terrazzo corridor to collect the leather. It afforded the boy a timeout of sorts, some minutes to contemplate the error of his ways before meeting his fate. The long walk to the office and back was gut churning.

One Brother ordered me to fetch the leather but to keep it out of sight of any parents or visitors to the school. 'Carry it up your sleeve,' he ordered. *Ingenious!* I thought. *Nobody will spot it there.* In my innocence, I felt that I was part of the plot. I was doing my teacher a favour. Teacher's pet. In effect, I was complicit in my own abuse. That's a habit that often stays with a child for a lifetime.

I never told my parents about the day in the schoolyard when I was summoned by a Brother who wasn't my teacher. It was just a few months since I had left Eason's Hill, where we spoke English to our teacher, and I momentarily forgot the language rules of the new regime.

I trotted over to the man in black who had called me and smiled. 'Yes, Brother?'

A lightning-fast hand shot out from the hip of his soutane and slammed straight into the side of my six-year-old head. I remember the feel of the wet concrete and my head going *whoozhe whoozhe whoozhe* as I struggled to make sense of where I was and what had just happened. This was my introduction to the sound of one hand clapping.

The champ standing over me snarled, '*Ná habair,* "Yes, Brother" *liomsa. Abair "Gabh mo leithscéal, a Bhráthair."*'

The blow to the head was merely a 'reminder'; my real punishment was to follow. He instructed me to stand at the base of the giant flagpole in the middle of the campus every morning of the following week. I was to be in position by five to nine and was to stand up straight and look directly ahead of me, as the Tricolour was raised to the strains of 'Amhrán na bhFiann' screeching from Tannoy speakers sprinkled across the campus. I did. I looked out through flooded eyes at over a thousand boys standing to attention and staring back at me.

As the daily humiliation went, so did my feelings. I went deep. I had to. I couldn't stay whimpering all week. The involuntary shaking and spasms had to stop.

By Friday, shame and embarrassment had given way to perverse pleasure, as I visualised crushing that Brother's head with a big fucking rock and then sticking one of my dad's screwdrivers into his eye and out the other side.

There was no way I was ever going to let my parents know that I had made a spectacle of myself. Every morning of that week and every week afterwards, I came up the ramp that led into the yard with a pain in my stomach that felt like a hunger pang. I'm not sure that knot in my gut has ever fully unravelled. Like the humming of a fridge in a kitchen, we learn to live with anxiety and don't notice it until it's plugged out. My knot in the stomach has been a constant companion. I've carried my public humiliation privately. It's in every chapter of my story. It's still something I feel isn't worth writing about, especially when I consider the horrendous injustice and savagery being meted out to children all over the planet in this very hour.

I continued to struggle at the books. Because my parents were overloaded with work and other responsibilities, I was able to hide it. I never showed them the red biro marks all over my copybooks, and if they ever enquired how school was going, I'd bamboozle them with positivity, all of it invented.

However, my end-of-year report was posted home and my mother's frown was enough for me to know that the truth always comes out. At the end of a long list of low scores and zeros, or 'duck eggs', as my dad called them, was the synopsis:

'This boy's heart is in the right place, but he is talkative, easily distracted and is falling behind with his work.'

Well, at least the bit about 'this boy's heart' was good.

ooo

The best part about school was the walk home. My school friends Tony Bullman and Gerard Healy were always good for a detour. We'd slog apples and have endless adventures in a row of derelict houses across from St Vincent's Girls' School. We were always welcome in Rea's shoe shop at the bottom of Broguemakers Hill. They were related to Seanie Carr and knew I was his next-door neighbour. Sometimes they'd even let you have a go at using the foot pedal on the sole press, a machine that slams down on the leather.

We all loved the crush in John's sweet shop before and after school. Hundreds of boys would struggle to elbow their way through the door to spend their pennies before the bell went. It was my introduction to crowd-surfing. John, the shop owner, loved the excitement himself and would unexpectedly chant snatches of the Latin Mass to the swaying heave of snotty-nosed schoolboys inside and outside the door. 'Come on! Make up your mind! No, they're two for a penny! We're out of 'em. Hey! Get down off that counter, you!' Then, without warning, he'd break into Gregorian Chant. 'DOME-EE-NUS

VOE-BIS-CUM!' he'd call, with outstretched arms. The Norrie equivalent of the Vienna Boys' Choir would observe one silent beat before the entire chorus of saucy Cork accents would rise in crescendo with the appropriate response: 'ET CUM SPIR-IT-TOO-TOO-OHO!'

Latin and Biblical references flavoured many of the conversations of my childhood. When one of us would eventually arrive sleepy-headed downstairs in the morning, my father would likely declare, 'The Dead arose and appeared to many,' and my mother would say, 'We've been calling you for *saecula saeculorum*.' Good news, like the safe birth of a baby, elicited a '*Deo gratias*', and I remember my father reckoning that our neighbour Mossie Sheehan was 'as old as Methuselah'.

Older boys would meet over at the Ramp or the Lodge gate, entrances on the far side of the school campus, which led to the secondary and technical schools. Long hair hadn't arrived in Ireland yet; fashion was still slick and so were Mon Boys like my brother Don. I'd often see him and his friends with their sharp haircuts and reefer jackets smoking cigarettes down at Miss Cahill's shop beside the Lodge gate. Once or twice I called in and bought a loose Carroll, a cigarette sold singly. If I was saving it for after school, I'd ask Don for 'a match and a scratch' from his box of matches and hide them in a pencil case I kept hidden under a rock in one of the derelict houses across from the girls' school.

I was swept away by the songs we learned in school. Heartbreaking historical ballads like 'Boolavogue', 'The Dying Rebel', and stirring marches that we sang as we stomped around the schoolyard: 'As young Roddy McCorley goes to die on the bridge of Toome today ...'

Like most of my mates, my stated ambitions were to play for Cork and to die for Ireland. One or the other would do, but the two feats were not mutually exclusive. Brother Desmond, a Limerick man, told us about James Dalton of Limerick who had done both. He had won an All-Ireland medal with Limerick in 1896 and was subsequently killed by the Brits during the War of Independence. Our new taoiseach, Jack Lynch, was a past pupil and had a couple of All-Ireland medals. Brother Desmond told us Jack was unlikely to die for Ireland, but anything was possible yet.

I loved hurling and I loved my hurley. I'd puck anything that wasn't nailed down. A stone, an apple core, a ball of tired chewing gum would be flaked over the wall, any wall. But the truth of the matter was that I wasn't much good at it. I suppose I had nobody to teach me the rules or the finer points. Don didn't play and my father hadn't time.

I remember the first match I played in the Old Mon Field. I was in second class and was told to 'go in at left corner forward', whatever that meant. One of the other boys told me where to stand. And I did ... I stood there for the whole first half. The action was all down the other end and the sliotar never entered our airspace. At half-time, the Brother mixed up the teams a bit, but told me to stay in my position. When the second half began, I returned to my position and within a few minutes the sliotar broke to me and I flaked it towards the goal, ran after it and flaked it again. Over the goal line it went to shouts of 'Creedon, you eejit. That's your own goal!' I never knew teams swapped sides at half-time, and so I managed to put one past our new goalkeeper. I've scored a few own goals in my lifetime, but that was the first.

Putting the Fist into Pacifist

In 1964, Cassius Clay became World Heavyweight Champion by beating Sonny Liston. He converted to Islam and changed his name from Cassius Clay, which he described as a 'slave name', to Muhammad Ali.

The following year, I started at the North Mon. I dropped my 'slave name' John Creedon and took on the ancestral version – Seán Ó Críodáin. I was renamed, not by the Muslim Brotherhood, but by the Christian Brotherhood.

Everyone in our house loved Muhammad Ali. You just had to. He was world champ. He was handsome. He was funny. He spoke up for poor people and he didn't take any bull from bullies. My mother said he was a 'conscientious objector', which meant he wouldn't go out to the war in Vietnam. He got into trouble for it.

I wished Ali could come to school with me because, apart from cross Christian Brothers and their straps, there were other dangers. Most days the walk home from school was more of a run home from school, especially if Todger was around.

Todger was eight years old and the biggest boy in the class. He had two little eyes buried deep in his chubby cheeks and had pimples on his forehead. Whenever he got cross, his chubby cheeks turned red and then he cried.

He wasn't fast, but if he cornered you, the options were either 'week in hospital' or 'sudden death' – the names he gave to his left and right fists. He usually approached me from behind when I was talking to someone else. It was always too late when I became aware of his presence, written on the frightened face of the kid in front of me.

Once, when he asked Brother McGettigan what part he was getting in the school Nativity play, McGettigan sized him up ... and then dismissed him with 'Bethlehem'. Everyone in the class burst their holes laughing, except Todger, who turned red, cried and kicked the head off me outside the school gates.

I really needed to toughen up. I was beginning to question how useful I would be to Cork in Croke Park or to Ireland in the GPO. But violence begets violence, so on it went.

'Did you take my *lón*?'

'Naw, I didn't touch it.'

'Why? Something wrong with my *lón*, is there? Something wrong with my mam's jam sandwiches, is there? Think you're great 'cause your mam owns a shop, do you?'

Todger never waited for an answer; he just kept piling on the accusations until the answers to all his own questions became evident to him. His cheeks turned purple, his eyes narrowed, and he continued. 'Think your mam is better than my mam 'cause she gives you ham sangwidges, do ya? Here, have your mam's ham sangwidges now, ya little spoilt fucker!'

In a face-washing motion, he mashed the bread and butter and cooked ham all over my face. 'Run home to your mother, ya little queer.' A bit harsh for a small child.

I confided in my sister Marie-Thérèse, who offered a solution to the daily attacks. 'Next time he shows up outside school, just sing "sticks and stones may break my bones, but names will never hurt me" and walk away.'

I did. And she was right. The name-calling stopped immediately; it was sticks and stones every day after that. Bricks too. One day, he showed up at the row of derelict houses by the Lodge gate and fired a brick that hit me on the back of the head.

A common way of coping with bullying is to normalise it. You'd kind of laugh along at the hilarious nicknames he would come up with. He'd call you a queer, so you'd mimic a woman's walk. The teacher would call him Bethlehem, so we'd have a right good snigger. His dad flakin' him, his mam flakin' him, him flakin' me, the Brother flakin' the two of us, me flakin' a young fella with glasses from a class down – sure, it was just one big 'the way it is'.

Some days I got home from school covered in blood and muck, but I would rather lie to my mother and tell her I was playing football than admit to losing another fight. You know how it is with boys and their mams. So I decided I was going to become like our hero Muhammad Ali and learn how to box.

I even wrote to Santy for a pair of Muhammad Ali boxing gloves. They were deadly and had helped Ali become the world champ. I saw the ad for them in a comic. The gloves were red and had 'Everlast' written around the lace-up wristband and Ali's autograph printed right where I wanted them to connect with any bully's jaw. They were lethal.

In the lead-up to Christmas, I sent the letter to the North Pole and started training in preparation for Christmas Day and the Judgement Day that would follow. My dad told me to swallow two raw eggs in a half a cup of milk every morning for strength, so I did. Gulp gulp. I started to run on the spot in our backyard, after which I would stick my head under the cold-water tap to cool down and toughen up. It's what the trainer did for the champ in between rounds.

I invited my dad out to my training camp in the backyard and asked him to teach me his tricks and techniques. He once beat up 12 Black and Tans with his bare hands and he had all the knacks. They read like a cocktail menu. There was the 'sidewinder' – a fist to the side of the head delivered with a final twist of the wrist. There was the 'uppercut', the 'reminder' and the *'paltóg'* – a heavy thump. The *'habhaistín'* was a direct blow to the opponent's head and there was a whole range of defensive measures too. *Cosain!* (block!), *seachain!* (duck!) And if worst came to worst and the sport of gentlemen descended into a free-for-all, you always had the 'cow's lash' – a backwards kicking action delivered in the general direction of the assailant as you retreated.

As my father grabbed his work bag and made for the door he said, 'Good luck with training now, and always remember that at the end of the day, *is fearr rith maith ná drochsheasamh*. A good run is better than a bad stand. So don't get into any unnecessary fights.' Then he added, 'Discretion is the better part of valour.' He always said that.

I practised combinations of blows, defensive moves and fancy footwork over and over again until they were coming naturally to me, like a *kata*. The moves were fast and furious and resembled a combination of *sean-nós* dancing and bare-knuckle boxing. '*Paltóg! Habhaistín! Cosain!* Uppercut! Two reminders left! And right! *Seachain!* Uppercut! Cow's lash! Run!'

Over and over again. I was duckin' and divin' even when I was having my dinner. My mother didn't know what was going on with me, but I couldn't afford to tell her. This was man stuff and she'd only try to stop me. All I needed was the super-charged Muhammad Ali gloves and I'd be invincible.

Christmas morning came. I got 'em!

Man oh man, they smelt beautiful, just like a new leather schoolbag. I squeezed my hands into each glove and discovered for the first time that you cannot lace up a boxing glove if you're already wearing one. But Eugenia helped me and I left them on for the day. My Christmas dinner went cold as I struggled with the cutlery, but I was preoccupied anyway, strutting around the house shadow-boxing at the hall mirror like I was Ali himself. 'Float like a butterfly, sting like a bee. Your hands can't hit what your eyes can't see.' Shimmy, duck, counter-punch. 'Yessss!'

I couldn't wait to go next door to Seanie Carr's. Seanie always said he didn't believe in Santy, so how was he going to explain where these came from? Hah?

He didn't say. But he was definitely impressed when I called to his door the next day and showed him.

'Why don't we have a sparring match?' I suggested as I followed him into his empty front room.

'Yeah, but you only have one pair.'

'What?'

'You only have one pair of boxing gloves,' he explained. 'Sure, what kind of present is that to get? Unless you live on a desert island and want to beat yourself up, one pair of boxing gloves is about as useful as a one-legged Granda Carr in an arse-kicking contest. Useless!'

'We can share them,' I countered. 'One glove each would be fair, wouldn't it?'

'It would,' said Seanie, taking the right glove.

'But that's my good hand!'

'You'll be grand,' he assured me.

I tied his glove for him and then slipped the other glove onto my own left hand. Space was tight in the Carrs' front room, so we moved the chairs out of the way and Seanie made the sound of a bell. We squared up to each other and began to circle.

I thought I'd lead off with a *paltóg* from my left. It was my weaker hand, but I had Muhammad Ali's glove. I let fly and BANG! I hit the floor as Seanie's uppercut landed on my jaw.

I wouldn't have minded, but it wasn't even the hand with the super-powered glove; it was his bare fist. He had floored me inside 10 seconds and I had no idea where I was. Lying on the flat of my back, I could see a ceiling bulb shining down on me, followed by Seanie's head looking down on me. 'Sorry 'bout that, kid. Get up or my mam will kill me. You've knocked the geranium off the window. She'll blow a gasket.'

He helped me to my feet, but my head was spinning and I thought my jaw was surely broken. He ushered me out into the hall. 'G'wan out the back and stick your head under the tap while I try and sweep up the mess you made. The cold water will fix ya.'

I stumbled down the back hall and tumbled out the back door into Rex's jaws. Seanie's cocker spaniel locked on to the calf of my right leg and wouldn't let go. I tried flaking him with the Muhammad Ali hand, but I was all over the place and I landed on the concrete just as Seanie ran out and hunted him.

I limped home in ribbons. My mother sent my sister with me up to the North Infirmary for a tetanus shot. I hadn't been in there since Blessed Martin nearly killed me. I told the nurse everything. I don't actually remember getting the injection, but I will always remember the year St Stephen's Day became Boxing Day and I became a conscientious objector.

Ballybunion

Baby brothers are the berries. A mother's love is a blessing and a sister's love is unconditional ... but a baby brother is the berries. I mean, you can't be wrestling your sister, but you can let your baby brother get you in a tiny headlock, groan for mercy and then pretend you've fainted. You can pretend you're a dinosaur and chew his chubby arm until he's convulsed with laughter. Then do it again and again until he nearly faints.

No one wanted to play toy soldiers with me until Cónal arrived. Don was nine years older than me and the girls weren't interested in shooting Nazis and blowing up Japanese airfields. They just didn't get it.

I had a two-year, two-stone advantage on Cónal, but I really wanted to play with him, so I would always endeavour to even up the score. When staging our World Wrestling Final in the kitchen, Morgan of the Mountains and the Tiny Terror would enter the ring wearing only our underpants. Circling my opponent while slapping my thighs and bellowing threats, I made a very convincing Morgan of the Mountains. But the second I turned my back to put a cat out of the ring, the Tiny Terror would rush me from behind with a tiny forearm smash that would leave me collapsed in a heap, moaning things like

'Please don't get me in a headlock.' The Tiny Terror was small, but he was smart, so he would take the hint and get me in a headlock, leaving me to slap the floor and groan, 'Submit. Submit.'

Same with Belly-Bashing Finals, when we would run at each other, hands behind the smalls of our backs, bellies out and ... BASH! until someone ended on the seat of their short pants.

My mother would regularly instruct us to take a run around the block 'to knock the tasp out of ye'. Smallies always got odds. So, once the shortest pair of legs had disappeared around Tommy Connell's corner at the bottom of our street, the next kid took off, and when he had disappeared, I'd flake off, wondering how far ahead they were. Once they came into sight, I had the measure of it and would pace my 'kick' to vary the results. I learned the hard way that if you didn't keep everyone in with a chance of winning, the game is up.

When Cónal and I shared a room, we'd spend hours talking, mostly about Christmas or planning some elaborate prank where I would dress Mother Cat in a tea towel and pretend she was Mother Teresa of Calcutta.

I was constantly inventing games and role play. 'Haul away, Charlie', a game inspired by the men shouting in McKenzie's yard, was a favourite. The bunkroom was perfect for this role play. We had a little wicker basket – a gondola, we called it. I tied a length of second-hand twine to the handle.

The twine had previously served its time binding one of the endless bundles of newspapers that were chucked at our shopfront from the open side door of a moving van in the middle of the night. The driver's assistant in the back of the News Brothers van could hit a shop door from a distance. With a back spin, the bundle would cling dead against the door, while the driver's assistant was already lining up the next bundle for Irene's shop up the street. My mother would always insist that we untie the twine or even the fine string of a coal bag rather than waste it. It would be coiled and stored in the top drawer in the shop. An exercise in thrift, acquired, no doubt, from her father and mother, who struggled to raise 10 girls on the side of a hill in 1920s Ireland. 'Bad cess to the war!' she would declare. 'De Valera closed the ports and my poor father couldn't sell a calf.'

Back in the bunkroom, we'd take turns at being 'Charlie'. Charlie was the winch operator in the top bunk, who would lower the basket over the side of the bed's pale enamel frame until it swayed beside the bottom bunk. The lowering would stop abruptly when the guy at the bottom would shout, 'Hould her steady, Charlie!' Then the man at the bottom, the loader, would place some mystery cargo into the wicker gondola, tug the string and shout, 'Haul away, Charlie!'

While the loader was the boss and shouted the instructions, Charlie, the crane operator, had the buzz of anticipation and the joy of surprise as the basket ascended, revealing its treasures. Usually, it was Seán Bunny, that soft, furry brown huggy-pal of my cradle days, who wore the same little blue dungarees with the patch pockets every day. Other times, Jingles, a slightly larger, less fluffy pink canvas rabbit in a crouched position, would arrive on the lift from ground zero, otherwise known as the ground floor. Jingles was borrowed from the girls' room; he had been Eugenia's hospital-bed partner from when she had a heart operation. Other times it could be Combat Johnnie, the poor boy's Action Man, which Santy only delivered to places like India, Africa and Ireland. On other occasions the payload from base camp might include a bag of Perri crisps, a small packet of chocolate buttons or a kitten. Kittens have an unflappable sense of balance, even in a swaying basket.

For a game of Wild Stallion, I would go down on all fours and Cónal, wearing his cowboy suit, would climb aboard, rodeo style. Saying, 'Hold onto my mane,' I would feel two little hands gripping the hair at the back of my head. 'Are you on properly?'

'I am. Go slow.'

'I will.'

'Promise?'

'Yeah!'

'OK so.'

Slowly, I'd begin to rotate, giving the occasional shudder, just to encourage the bareback rider to squeeze with his knees like I had already warned him. By bending my elbows a little, the rider was rocked forward, and by arching my back he was knocked back. As I increased the intensity of the ride, I compensated with Wild West words of encouragement. 'Yes siree, you're good at this, pardner! Wow, I'll bet this kid has broken in his share of wild stallions in his day!' The whoopin' and hollerin' of the kid subsided in direct relation to the intensity of the ride. By the time I was raising my front hands off the floor, the rider was more focused on staying the course than whoopin' and hollerin'.

One day when playing with toy soldiers, I got another of my bright ideas. My dad's navy bus driver's hat with the black patent peak looked just like a Nazi general's hat. My sister Connie had a navy gaberdine she wouldn't miss if I borrowed it, and there were numerous girls' school berets in the sock drawer. So I quickly 'wrote' a play about the French Resistance and their struggle against the Nazis, who were even worse than the Brits. We could stage it across the road in Mossie Sheehan's front room. My parents had bought the house after Mossie died with the intention of letting it out. My dad had knocked down the interior walls of the little shop and had finished decorating the house, so it now had a huge front room with three windows.

I dragged about twelve chairs across from our kitchen and sitting room. Everyone at home had to eat standing up for a day or two, but that was a small price to pay for my big opening night. Furthermore, Mam said I could and she was the boss of all of us. Her workload was overwhelming, she hadn't a moment to herself, but any artistic endeavour at all had her full support.

After much scribbling in my copybook, eventually the page with the script and stage directions was ready. I was to be the Nazi general who stumbles into an ambush. Cónal, Henry Condon and Dónal Sweeney were to be the entire French Resistance, who were going to jump out from behind a couch screaming, '*Vive la France!*' – which, coincidentally, was the only line in the entire play. I was free to improvise with '*Achtung!*' or '*Arrrgh!*' or whatever I felt was appropriate at the moment of my death.

We already had a plastic machine gun that fired plastic silver bullets. Ironically, I had won the machine gun in a 'Safety First' competition in the *Cork Examiner*. We also had a cowboy pistol that held a roll of caps, which banged loudly when fired. I would take the pistol, as befits a general. My good new machine gun was entrusted to Cónal because he knew how to fire it, and the lads brought their own guns and ammo.

Geraldine, who was in art college at the time, was my head of wardrobe, make-up and props. She distributed the school berets and made three neckerchiefs to make the lads look more French, before painting a moustache on each of their faces as a final touch. I asked her to give me a moustache too, but she said that a moustache, as well as the bus driver's hat, would make me look too much like Hitler. I also asked her to help me open out a huge cardboard box and turn it into the general's Mercedes. She did. She even put a little handle on the inside so I could glide my own prop across the 'stage' as if it were a moving car, all the while holding my dad's binoculars to my eyes with my right hand as if surveying the hills for French pig-dogs.

There was a full house for opening night, which was on a Saturday afternoon. The chairs were occupied by my sisters, Aunty Theresa and Seanie Carr. There were also a few kids from the street standing behind the chairs.

The cue for the French Resistance to attack was to be the moment I put down the binoculars, as if I was satisfied that the '*schweinhunds*' could not possibly be hiding behind the couch. In fairness, right on cue, the French Resistance came out all guns blazing and all caps banging, screaming '*Vive la*

France!' exactly as we had rehearsed. That was actually the name of the play: *Vive la France*.

As the three-minute drama reached a climax and I lay dying inside the cardboard box, the audience started to giggle at my efforts. I looked out over the box as if to say, 'There's no need to take that attitude. What's so funny, ye assholes?' I flung off my busman's hat and stormed backstage in an embarrassed rage worthy of Zero Mostel in *The Producers*.

By the following day, I was over the hurt of my first-ever flop and back to press-ganging Cónal into some other caper.

ooo

On a handful of occasions, my father brought both of us to work. He landed a handy overtime shift driving the Ballybunion bus on Saturdays. Cork to Ballybunion was 82 miles by car or 104 miles by bus. Allowing for stops in places such as Rathmore and Listowel, the meandering bus journey took about four hours each way. The day trip to Bally was a 14-hour shift for my dad and for us. We loved it. Ballybunion was like some place from the *Beano* and we were like the Bash Street Kids. There was a beach, bingo, candy floss, 99s and amusement arcades. It even had a funny name. My dad would call it 'Bally-Big-Bunion', 'Bally-Bingin' and 'Bally-B'.

Once he had parked the bus in the yard at the edge of town, the three of us would troop down to the women's beach for 'a dip in the ole briny', as Dad called it. On a good day, Ladies' Beach was awash with men, women and children splashing in the waves or just 'bamin' out in dere baydinas'. A beach full of red necks and white bodies absorbed in the seaside symphony of breaking waves, yelping children, screeching gulls and, somewhere in the distance, a transistor relaying Michael O'Hehir's commentary from Croke Park.

The Creedon boys were all very modest and would spend ages finding a quiet place to manoeuvre towels and togs while keeping our arses to the wall. You could hear Dad the length of the beach singing an old music-hall favourite of his from behind his towel: 'I'm shy, Mary Ellen, I'm shy'.

I'm shy, Mary Ellen, I'm shy
It does seem so naughty, oh, my!
Men are so rough and I'm sure they will stare
They'll splash me, and duck me, if I go in there
The girls ain't so rough as the men
They wouldn't duck me, or try
So I'd rather bathe here along with the girls
'Cause I'm shy, Mary Ellen, I'm shy!

We knew what the song was about, but we were too shy to laugh out loud, so we would splutter and turn away as we tried to maintain our modesty.

A plunge in the briny without a bag of chips afterwards is like Sunday dinner without a dessert. So, once we had shaken sand from crack and crevice, pulled our back-to-front underpants over our damp bums, squeezed out our sopping socks and coiled our togs and towels into Swiss rolls, we were off again. Up the hill to Main Street, starvin' for sausages and chips, after which Dad would take the big bag of wet togs and towels and head for the bus yard for a game of cards and a cup of tea with the other drivers from Limerick and Tralee.

Before he'd leave, he'd divvy out the bobs: a half-crown between two of us. We'd get change from the kiosk: two shillings and sixpence divided by two meant 'one and three' each. There was a bar of Cadbury's milk chocolate and an apple each, that Mother had given us, waiting for us back on the bus, so the money was all for the amusements. The bumpers cost a shilling, and whoever paid the man got to steer. If you were in early in the day, you'd get better mileage. As long as there weren't people waiting, you'd be left to float around the floor, sparks flyin' from the top of the electric antenna at the back, like some moving advertisement catching the eye of people walking past the door.

I dreamt of one day getting a job there, like the teenagers who stepped effortlessly from one moving car to another as they untangled pile-ups and traffic jams, mostly caused by people taking driving lessons from their dads. The woman in the cash kiosk said Nagle's Amusements was the biggest driving school in Ballybunion and that most people in North Kerry had learned to drive there.

If you won a few bob on the push-penny machine, you might manage the price of another go on the bumpers. If, someday, we got a massive payout, I was going to blow the lot and take the two of us on the Ghost Train. I would have loved to know what was beyond those swing doors that opened into the gaping mouth of the green and ugly witch painted on the wall. A boy in the arcade had told me one day that the ride was deadly. He said that the train didn't go very far, but that it felt like it did because you were in there for ages. But that remained a distant dream because we always left with empty pockets. Also, I couldn't very well go in and leave my little brother outside. I mean, what would my mother say if he was robbed by a murderer while I was living the high life inside on the Ghost Train. 'All for one and one for all!' was the motto we had adopted from the Three Musketeers in the *Look and Learn* magazines in the bunkroom.

However, on one occasion I was sent off with Dad to Ballybunion on my own. There was no one to play 'I

Spy' with on the bus and the dip in the briny wasn't great. I mean, you couldn't put your dad on your back and shout 'Ejector seat!' as I did every time I propelled my younger brother backwards into the air with the guarantee of a soft and salty landing. The sausages and chips and tea and bread weren't the same either without being able to say something funny to him and make him snort his tea all over our chips.

When Dad and I had finished the grub and it was time for us to head our separate ways for the afternoon, I suggested that I go with him to the seaweed baths.

'Yerra, you wouldn't like it at all.'

'I would.'

'Yerra, you wouldn't, there'd be a load of crabs inside in the weed in the bath.'

'What?'

'Erra, no, you'd have a grand afternoon up the town,' he groaned, as he leaned to one side, plunging his hand deep into his money pocket. 'Don't do anything stupid now and I'll see you above at the bus at four o'clock. And for Christ's sake, don't get lost or go off with anyone,' he concluded as he handed me a half-crown.

I was nodding along in agreement, although not one of his words landed. My head was already full with my own internal conversation. *A half-crown?* I thought, as the reality sank in. *A half-crown? The*

Ghost Train! I can go on the Ghost Train with a half-crown. I must stay calm until he stops talking and clears off to the seaweed baths.

Then down I went in giant strides to Nagle's Amusements, hoping to God they wouldn't be closed because of a death in the family or anything, because this opportunity would never EVER come again.

As I rounded the corner onto Main Street, I could hear the barrel-organ sound of Nagle's Amusement Arcade calling seductively to enter the pleasure dome. The usual guy with the Teddy-boy quiff was on duty, leaning on the counter, flicking half-heartedly through one of them English papers with the girls in them.

The Ghost Train was all lined up and ready to go. It had three little two-seater open carriages, all in wildly contrasting colours: turquoise, canary yellow and shocking pink.

I stood in front of the pay booth, looking up politely at the hatch.

The voice inside it spoke. 'Yeah?'

'Is the Ghost Train going?'

'Later.'

'Will I wait or come back?'

'Come back.'

'OK.'

I went for a walk off down by the old Central Ballroom, which had become the New Central

Ballroom, its exterior wall accommodating a balcony that bulged out over the footpath like a giant arse. A tattered poster on the wall gave me something to read before returning to check if the Ghost Train was ready for me. Squinting at the faded print on the torn and dog-eared poster, I could just pick out the large print:

'Announcing Gala Opening of New Central Ballroom. Thursday Next May 23rd. Celebrated author and playwright John B. Keane will perform the grand opening. One of our own! Dancing to Maurice Mulcahy Orchestra. Win a £100 note or other cash prizes. Mineral Bar. Admission 10/-.'

I made a note to tell my dad the news about the new dance hall. It might keep the Cork bus busy. I'd also tell him what John B. Keane had been up to since last year, when we saw him on the beach sunbathing with his family. A huge crowd of thousands of people were walking around them just having a look. I remember Dad was annoyed. Tutting about the invasion of privacy, he said, 'God forgive me my sins, but isn't it a fright to God and his Blessed Mother that the poor man can't take his family for a dip in the briny without being tormented?'

I didn't have a watch, but I estimated that an hour had passed since I left the man above at the Ghost Train. So back with me up to the arcade.

'Is the Ghost Train going now?'

'I told you five minutes ago that it's too early. Would you ever feck off for yourself and come back later?'

I fecked off down the town. I couldn't go into a pub like I would in Cork. You wouldn't know who might be in there. It could be the saucy young fellas from Limerick who threw rocks at us the year before.

I looked in the window of Mike's Gift Shop. They had a lovely tea towel with a map of Ballybunion and a load of facts down the side, with 'Souvenir of County Kerry' written on it in big green-and-yellow letters. I would have liked to get it for my mother as a present. She had loved the one I brought her back from the school tour to Youghal a few months earlier. She said it was her favourite tea towel and very handy too. But I needed the money for the Ghost Train and the hour was probably up now anyway.

When I got back, yer man looked up to heaven and said, 'You again!' I suppose he recognised me well at this stage.

'Yeah, is it OK to have a go on the train now?'

'Have you anyone with you?'

'No. I'm on me own.'

'Well, I'll have to wait until I get a few more customers, but go on, you can sit in and wait.'

I gave him the two shillings and raced to grab the best seat even though there was no one else around. I sat in the front carriage, staring straight ahead at the yawning mouth of those huge swing doors. The giant green witch had a horrible wart on her nose like the old bitch on the bicycle who robbed Toto in *The Wizard of Oz*. I looked over my shoulder at yer man to see if a crowd was gathering. Nothing.

I gave it another few minutes and then looked back at him again with a sad face and said, 'I have to be up to the Cork bus by four o'clock. Is it four o'clock yet?'

'Nearly,' says he. 'Do you want to go in on your own so altogether?'

'Yeah, that would be great 'cause I don't –'

Before I could finish my sentence, he had pulled the lever and I was catapulted through the witch's mouth and flung into the darkness, the double doors banging shut behind me.

The carriage rattled through the blackness. I could hear the dead screaming up ahead. Suddenly the face of the devil lit up right beside my face and screamed, 'You're mine! All mine!' I wouldn't normally curse, but I shouted, 'Fuck off!'

Then a spotlight picked out a skeleton standing on the train track right in front of me, but there was no stopping this thing, so my carriage crashed straight through him, and the skeleton landed in the seat beside me before falling off, cackling.

The noise of the train and the screaming of the ghosts was deafening, but I couldn't see beyond my nose. Without warning I went headlong into a load of spiderwebs hanging at face height from the ceiling. Shivers ran down my spine as the carriage tilted sideways and nearly flung me out, before a witch on a broomstick overhead spat 'Welcome to Hell!' as my face brushed against her trailing black cape. I really wanted this to stop and gasped, 'Please, Jesus, make this over nowww ... Ow!' A pair of hairy hands grabbed me by the throat and started strangling me. The hands were so big and strong that it had to be a gorilla or a yeti or something, but I didn't have time to think about that. I instinctively knew that I was going to be eaten alive if I didn't flake the shit out of him, so I swung the hardest *paltóg* I could muster over my shoulder in the general direction of the hairy hands. Because I was sitting and my assailant was probably standing, my clenched fist landed at about hip height in what felt like a soft area.

The strangling stopped immediately, but the train hurtled on through the darkness and the wailing of the dead. An unexpected shaft of daylight entered the dungeon from a door on the side wall and I glimpsed a man darting out. Within seconds I came crashing blindly through the exit to a sudden stop that nearly flung me out of the carriage.

I sat there, frozen, for what seemed like another hour, staring straight ahead, waiting for my insides to catch up with the rest of me.

Later, when the feeling came back into my little legs and I prepared to leave the carriage, I looked over at yer man, who was back behind the counter reading the paper as if nothing had happened. He looked up and said, 'Do you want another go?'

'Huh?'

'You can go in again for free if you want.'

'Nah. You're grand. Thanks very much.'

As I wobbled back up to the bus, using the wall for support, I thought, *If I ever ride that train again, I'll be bringing the entire French Resistance from Cork with me.*

Away with the Manger

Give me your tired, your poor,
Your huddled masses yearning to breathe free,
The wretched refuse of your teeming shore.
Send these, the homeless, tempest-tost to me,
I lift my lamp beside the golden door!

– Excerpt from 'The New Colossus', Emma Lazarus

My mother was Cork's Statue of Liberty. She was a beacon for the tired, the poor and the misunderstood who presented themselves at our shop counter. Every day brought something different: a student friend of one of my sisters who didn't have a place to stay, a warm cardboard box perforated with air holes with 'Whitaker's Day-Old Chicks' printed on the side, a pigeon with a broken wing that Marie-Thérèse found on Pine Street, even a little bonham that was bound for Adrigole on the Berehaven bus. The bonham, who we named Lily the Pig, stayed with us until an old neighbour collected her, put her in a box and delivered Lily to her final destination, to much sobbing in our kitchen. So a stray dog was par for the course.

When Louie Angelini from the betting office next door asked me to ask my mother if she wanted a dog, it was really like asking me to ask Christ if he wouldn't mind being crucified. You knew it wasn't fair but that there'd be little resistance. Similarly, the last thing my mother needed was another dog, but I knew she'd say yes, eventually.

'But Louie said he'll be going to the electric chair if he doesn't find a new owner,' I argued.

'Why can't Louie keep him himself?'

'He already has a dog.'

'So have we.'

'I know, but this fella is going to be killed,' I pleaded.

'Has he the mange?'

'Naw, he's perfect, and Louie said he's a great guard dog.'

Mange was like TB – you wouldn't want it in the house. A lot of people would throw stones at a dog and chase him away if he was a manger. Hannie Mac told my mother that one of the Cronins got mange off a stranger. On enquiry, we discovered that what Mrs Cronin had actually said was that one of her boys got mange from a *stray manger* who had pups above in Bell's Field. Except Mrs Cronin called it 'scabies' to sound posh. I knew the manger above in Bell's Field. She looked like a small greyhound. She was sad, skinny and missing clumps of fur. I felt sorry for her. I felt sorry for all mangers. There was one of them in the crib the night Jesus was born and he got on grand with all the sheep and the Holy Family and everyone.

'Pleeease can we keep him?' I begged. 'I'll mind him and feed him and do everything for him.'

'I don't know, pet. We'll have to ask Dad when he comes home. But he'll probably say no.'

Every boy deserves two things: a dog ... and parents who allow him to keep it. As it turns out, I had both. The deal was the same as every other time: 'Well, OK so, but only until we find him a home.'

Mick was an oul' dote – a middlin'-sized dog with a mass of heavy black curls and ringlets. Nobody really knew what Mick looked like under his carpet of dreadlocks, apart from the shine of his wet nose and the occasional glimpse of his glassy eyes laughing through the curly fringe that cascaded over his face. My mother decided he was a cross between a Kerry Blue and a poodle. He'd herd the day-old chicks all day and wiggle his hips with excitement when he saw me coming in the door from school. He could tell if I was sad or in trouble and would follow me out to the back stairs to sit beside me on the bottom step. But we soon discovered why Mick had been destined for death row.

Priests, bus drivers, guards, postmen, nuns, anything in a uniform was fair game for Mick. He loved children, but for some reason he hated authority. My father said he was like a cross between a cross terrier and Lassie. 'He'd ate the leg off you and then run for help.'

We had a visit from the dog warden. Mick had pulled a Christian Brother off his bicycle and was now on his last warning. My mother was reluctant to let Mick go to Clontarf Street for execution, so she put a sign in the shop window: 'FREE TO GOOD HOME, KERRY BLUE CROSS'. My dad said she should have put in a full stop after 'Kerry Blue'.

'Johnny Creedon is looking for a guard dog and said he'd be happy to have him,' she announced to me after school.

'But why can't we just keep him?'

'I know, peteen, but he'd be happier farmed out, herding the chickens below in Glounthaune, and Johnny said you can go down to visit him any time you want.'

Johnny Creedon was a bus driver and small farmer. Although we shared a name and he looked a little like my dad, we weren't related. Johnny was a good friend of the family and would call once a week to collect our household waste to feed his pigs: egg shells, stale bread, potato skins, tea leaves, the lot. I didn't know what he meant, but every time he'd finish loading the slop buckets into the boot of his black Morris Minor, he'd slam down the door and say, 'That's a grand cake now. Fatty Arbuckle will make short work of that. Christ, she'd ate the quarter sessions.' Johnny loved animals, but I was still heartbroken at the prospect of losing Mick to the farm, or worse, the other option.

On the way home from school, I told my best friend, Gerard Healy, about the choice I had to make. Mick was heading for death row unless I let Johnny take him to Glounthaune, where he couldn't bite anyone in a uniform. We walked slowly down Shandon Street, passing Broguemakers Hill – without calling into Rea's shoemakers – we had more pressing matters on our minds. Looking down at our feet solemnly, we avoided every crack on the pavement as we considered the conundrum before us.

'Remember what Brother Gill told us about Hobson's choice and what that means?' asked Gerard.

'I do. No choice, really.'

'Exactly, and you can't run away from home with Mick – that would be stupid.'

We turned left at the North Gate Bridge and onto Pope's Quay, where we found an empty bench. Usually there were two old dossers in flat caps and navy dungarees sitting there. Everyone called them 'Cha' and 'Miah'. They must have found a day's work somewhere because the bench was free. We unhitched our schoolbags and rested our backs, admiring the new Cork Opera House on the far side of the Lee.

Gerard had twopence, so we bought a pair of apples from Mrs Murphy, a shawlie who sold fruit from her barrow at the end of Carroll's Quay. She looked noble, like a Navajo woman, with her black tassel shawl and big hoop earrings framing a loose bun of white hair and a tanned complexion from decades of facing south to the sun.

Gerard suggested we detour from our usual route and follow the tide towards the harbour. We followed the one-sided Georgian terrace, Camden Quay, along Patrick's Quay and across Brian Boru Bridge to Clontarf Street Dogs' Home. The big iron gate was always kept firmly locked and bolted, but there was a kind of hatch set into the wall where you could look into the yard and see what dogs were in stock. It was sort of a poor man's zoo, always worth a quick peep on your way past in case there was a huge wolfhound or maybe boxer puppies on view. There was a tortoise in there once.

As we tippy-toed to see in the hatch, Gerard gave me his fanciful version of how they executed dogs in Ireland. 'Y'see the shed over there to the side?'

'Yeah.'

'That's where they do it. The man goes out into the yard and calls the dog, all nice and sweety-pie-like, as if they're going to bring him on his holidays.'

'G'way.'

'Yeah, he'd pretend he had a bag of sweets in his hand or something, and when the poor dog'd follow him into the shed, he'd slam the door behind the two of 'em. Then he'd murder him.'

'How?'

'They have a big sheet of galvanised metal on the floor with wires coming out of it and into a big switch up on the wall. The man'd throw the sweet onto the sheet of metal and when the dog steps onto it, he'd pull down the big switch and the dog do be fried to the spot. My dad says you'd even get a smell of cooking out on the street when they're doing it.'

'Bloody basters!'

I went straight home and told my mother that Johnny Creedon could have Mick.

Even though I was heartbroken, I told Mick it was for the best. Johnny had a great way with dogs and even remembered not to wear his CIÉ uniform on the day he came to collect him. He saw that I was down in the dumps and assured me that I was welcome to come to Glounthaune and visit Mick any time. I shrugged and said, 'Sure.'

My mother and father were delighted and said, 'Great!' To put it simply, my parents were flahed out, so Mick and myself were farmed out.

Not unlike Mick, I suppose I too was a handful. It's not that I set out to be bold – I just couldn't keep my nose out of anything, including pubs. When my sisters were sent out to search for me they could find me anywhere: on a building site, a bus … once they even found me on a French navy boat down the docks. I was more a danger to myself than anyone else. My mother pined for the countryside of her childhood and insisted that she didn't want to see her children 'dragged up on the side of the street', as she put it.

And so it began. Summer holidays and weekends, I was sent to the country. *Grand*, I thought. *It'll be an adventure and at least I'll get to see Mick again.*

Farmed Out

Johnny Creedon had one brown arm and one white arm. Like my dad, he was a bus driver and, whatever the weather, his right elbow rested upon the open window of his Leyland 38-seater as it ground its way northwards through Knockraha in the morning and freewheeled much of the homeward journey in the evening, its inner wing mirror swishing the fuchsia, just for the craic.

This particular morning, with his trouser braces dangling behind him, Johnny scraped away at the white bristles on his chin. He was thinking of turning hay. The sun was up early and already a shaft of sunlight poured in over the half door and warmed his back. On the shelf, beside the Midleton Co-op Mart calendar, the medium-wave wireless hummed a housewives' favourite tune.

This cosy cottage scene imploded as my panic-stricken voice yelped over the half door. 'Quick, Johnny, quick! Teresa McGonagle has escaped from the shed and is running for the main road!'

'D'oulfuckinhure!' said Johnny under his breath, as he whipped the towel from his shoulder and simultaneously grabbed a coil of rough rope from its hook by the fire. 'Quick, willyu. Head up over Pollanarigid and block the bitch. If she makes it to the back road we'll never catch her. That lightin' hure has my heart broken.'

Teresa McGonagle was 19 years old and the eldest of the three cows in Johnny's herd. Teresa was a natural matriarch and the queen of escapology. She knew exactly how to time her run. Never with a full udder … never. She'd always wait until after milking. Then, with her load lightened, she'd bolt for the door of the shed. Once a safe distance from her pursuer, she would down gears from a headlong gallop to a triumphant sashay, only to take off again if the invisible line of safety was breached.

Later, as Johnny led Teresa back into the haggard with the rough rope around her horns, I kept the rearguard at a safe distance, armed with a sally rod.

'The cow's lash is an awful man, isn't it, Johnny? It could kill a grown man stone dead before he even knew what hit him. Isn't that right, Johnny?'

'Tis.'

'Maybe we should sell her, Johnny, get rid of her. I'd say you'd get a load of money for her, 'cause she's so big an' all. And she was a great milker in her day, wasn't she, Johnny?'

No reply.

'Or maybe we should change her name to Teresa McGone-Again? That'd be a right good joke, Johnny, wouldn't it?'

'Should call her Houdini,' Johnny grumbled to himself.

'What's that? She has your heart broken, Johnny, hasn't she?'

Johnny's heart had never been broken. He wouldn't let it. If he ever loved anything, it was the 14 acres he farmed at Lackenroe in Glounthaune: a patchwork of nine fields and a haggard, stitched together by the intricate lacework of a long-dead dry-stone waller. Johnny worked hard to juggle the farming with the bus-driving, but now his younger namesake from the city could attend to some of the day-to-day chores and Mick would be a handy guard dog while Johnny was at work.

By comparison, my feelings about the arrangement were mixed. I had already had many wonderful day trips to my cousins' farm in Adrigole. Aunty Kit and her husband Jack Michael would spoil us. We'd help saving the hay and bringing in the cattle at milking time. Our cousins Ronnie and Denis would bring us all outside at night and we would stare upwards in awe at the twinkling night sky over Bantry Bay with Jack's binoculars. Denis taught me some great football knacks and we once drank a full bottle of Cidona.

This was different. There were no kids, just Johnny and me, and I'd be expected to take care of the farm on my own when Johnny was at work. Still,

I could practise being a farmer-priest and at least I would be with Mick every day.

Lackenroe was a Noah's ark of variety, where every animal had its place and its name. There were three German shepherds: Amber, Linda and Lassie. They were kept in an old barn in case they'd stray and only let out for a gallop when Johnny was around. There were three donkeys: Rosie, Deirdre and Deirdre's foal, Philip. The milking parlour was the preserve of Teresa McGonagle and her two ladies-in-waiting, Clare and the Blue Cow. And now a certain Kerry Blue called Mick had the run of the house.

In the haggard there were six pigsties in a row. That's where Fatty Arbuckle and the other breeding sows and their bonhams lived. There were always a few 'dry cattle' of various breeds in stock. Johnny referred to them as a mixed herd because of their different colours and they didn't have names because they would be going off to Midleton Mart. The residents of the hen house didn't have names either, apart from the eldest, Henrietta, who ruled the roost. The hens were terrorised by the cock, who didn't really have a name either, but Johnny said the hens referred to him as 'Casanova' after a famous film. I had never seen the film myself.

In my weekly letter home, I wrote,

Dear Mammy and Daddy. I hop you are fine. I am good too. I think Johnny is fibbing agin. He said the hens were watching the televisin up stairs. But there is no televisin here. Their is no upstairs here too. He said he just heard them talking. Johnny can talk hen and cow. I saw him at it myself but he says theres no talking to donkeys because they just won't listen. Johnnie will bring me home on Sunday. Can I come down agin for the hay? Tell everyone I love them.

*Yours sincerely,
Mister John Creedon Junor*

Johnny was right about most things, including the proven fact that there is no talking to donkeys. 'If a donkey doesn't want to move, that's it. You're stuck. Some lads take the rod to them, but that's no guarantee either,' he emphasised.

He went on: 'I saw an old bollox over at the creamery one day. He was offloading churns of milk onto the delivery stand, and try as he might, he couldn't get his donkey to budge when the job was finished. Now, there was a procession of horses and carts behind them, all queueing for the stand. So, *mo dhuine* gave his oul' donkey a few good hard cracks of the sally rod on the rump, but she wasn't for moving.

'The next thing was, our bould bucko got up off the cart and came around to the front of the donkey and hit her one right *paltóg* into the muzzle with his closed fist. Well, the donkey bit him down on the shoulder and would ... not ... let ... go. Your man was left roaring and trying to punch her with the left hand. But I tell you, that donkey was a right match for any southpaw. Every time your man swiped, the donkey ducked and nearly tore the shoulder out of the socket. Well, if the donkey hadn't taught him a lesson that day, someone else would eventually. Shaggin' tramp!'

'What did you do?' I asked, enthralled.

'Well, in the heel of the hunt, I bought the donkey off him and that was the end of that.'

'Which one? Rosie or Deirdre?'

'Rosie's mother. You never met her. She was cross enough, mind.'

'Does Rosie look like her mother?'

'The head off her and stubborn like her too. *Briseann an dúchas trí shúile an chait.* She had no name up to then, only "the dunkey", so I called her Mamie after an old aunt of mine. Either way, there's no talking to donkeys. They understand every single word you're saying, but they'll make up their own minds about it.'

Johnny had great stories about animals and I loved hearing them. Mick and myself liked being farmed out to him. Sometimes, he might give out to us, but he never hit his animals or me.

On occasion I got homesick, but that was usually only at night, or if Johnny came home later than I expected. Mostly, I loved being the boss of myself and the animals all day. If ever Johnny asked me was I OK, I'd say, 'Grand,' and he'd always laugh and say, 'Why wouldn't you? Good food and pleasant surroundings.' He always said that when he talked about Lackenroe.

ooo

The regime was tough but fair. I had chores to do while Johnny was on the bus run. I'd collect the eggs from the hen house and wash them. I'd stand on an old milk crate to reach the handle of the mangel grinder, a big old cast-iron contraption for shredding mangels. Mangels are a large root crop that look like turnips on the outside, but they emerge from the bottom of the grinder as snow-white chips as crisp as an apple, lined with a fine raspberry-ripple stripe. They're used for animal feed, but I once asked Johnny if he had ever tasted a mangel. He never answered me, but one day when he was away at work, I tried a chip off of one. I never told anyone what I did and it would be hard to describe the taste. You'd really have to try it for yourself.

If the handle of the grinder had been left in the up position by Johnny, then I'd have a right stretch to reach it. With both hands clenched around the cold handle that had long lost its rubber grip, I'd step off the milk crate and dangle from the handle. It took all of my six-stone weight to get it to slowly creak and begin a full revolution. Once 'twas going, 'twas grand, and Johnny often said the same about me. He'd always tell people, 'John's a great little worker once he gets going, but 'tis hard to get him goin'!'

Johnny had no relations nearby and no family that he ever spoke about to me. Sometimes he would introduce me as 'my namesake', and once in Midleton Mart a man said, 'Is your son helping you today?' and before I could say anything, Johnny said, 'He is.'

We loved a spin into Midleton for the mart or over the road to the Sugarloaf for the messages. The Sugarloaf was a pub run by Mr Deasy. It had a shop on the side managed by his wife, Mrs Deasy, and petrol pumps outside run by their son, Greasy Deasy. Johnny would be whistling at the wheel and I'd be on the passenger seat with Mick, all the windows open. Mick loved standing on his hind legs, facing the breeze through the open window with my arm around him, tongue flopped to one side, tasting the air. And I loved the way the wind would part the mop of curls on his shaggy fringe and we would get a rare glimpse of those glassy eyes.

Mick followed me everywhere and I loved that. Johnny left strict instructions: 'If a strange van comes into the haggard, just tell them that the dog is mad and they'd better stay in the van. If they get out, you can leave the rest of it to Mick. Just go in and lock the door until Mick is finished with them.'

On the farm, I would clean out the sties and troughs and top up the pig ration. I'd give a couple of fists of hay and half a bucket of mangels to each of the three cows and two adult donkeys. I'd feed and lock up the hens for fear of the fox or, worse, Casanova. Once the haggard gate was secured for the night with the loop of rope, my compadre Mick and myself would take our chores indoors.

Using all my strength, I'd lift the big black cauldron off the ground, groaning and straining until I eventually flipped its noisy handle over the crook that jutted out of the stonework over the open fire. Then, using a cracked blue and white milk jug from the mixed herd of crockery on the dresser, I would transfer several pints of water from the enamel bucket into the big witch's pot. Next, two newspapers were taken from the pile that was stacked well away from the open fire. The leftover newspapers were brought from our shop whenever Johnny collected me or the household waste. Broadsheets were best, because the newspapers had to be spread out in a big square on the stone floor for the final task of the day, which was conducted by Johnny himself. So, until the boss got home, we would have to sit tight.

As dusk crept in the window and the air cooled, the arthritic joints of the cottage would creak. Mick and myself would cock an ear at the slightest sound and then dart an eye at one another for reassurance.

Eventually, quoting the boss, I'd sigh and say, 'Idle hands are the divil's work. C'mon, Mick, we'll get the ould fire going.' I'd build a pyramid of dry cippins and a few twists of the *Cork Examiner*. Another strip of paper would make a handy fuse, and a couple of long thin sods of dry turf would provide a base for the blocks of timber to come once we had ignition. By now, it was as good as dark outside, but eventually the yellow glow of Johnny's headlights would illuminate the fuchsia hedgerows along the lane.

With the welcome click-click of the latch lifting and falling, Johnny was in. Carrying an old canvas bag over his shoulder, he would greet Mick and myself with a simple 'How're the men?' The bag's contents would be spilled onto the waiting newspapers. The severed heads of two cows and three or four sheep would tumble onto the papers, their contorted expressions staring as if they were blinded by the sudden light.

Using a builder's shovel, Johnny would scoop up each head with the skill of a Cork hurler and egg-and-spoon it into the bubbling cauldron. An hour later, Johnny would lift the weighty cauldron off the hook and drag the heads out of the beige water with coal tongs and a poker. The smell was like the smell of stew in Hannie Mac's house and I sometimes wondered if that was how Mick would have smelt if they had got him on the electric chair. Once, when Johnny lifted the lid, there was a huge eyeball being tossed around the surface by the bubbling beige water. The boys in school didn't believe me when I told them that happened, but it did.

Johnny would sharpen the two carving knives with a few swipes on the stone step outside the back door and then hand me the one with the good handle. The first few times I had to cut the meat off the heads I nearly got sick, but after a while I got used to it. The cheek was the easiest bit and you could cut the ear off handy enough, but there wasn't much meat on it. I hated when I had to touch the animals' lips or bristles, but the German shepherds would wolf the lot of it.

I never got used to feeling sorry for the poor cows and sheep, though. I often thought about how I would hate it if Johnny ever sold Teresa McGonagle to the knacker's yard.

After we had washed up, we had our own grub. Johnny used to say it was goats' heads and mangels on my plate, but I knew it wasn't. I think it was mostly bacon and turnips and spuds. Sometimes it was a fry. We always had dessert, usually tinned pears or peaches set in cold custard. Other times we had rhubarb and custard. We never had ice cream because Johnny had no fridge – he used to say it was upstairs with the telephone, the toilet and the television.

Dessert was one of my favourite things about Lackenroe, and afterwards there would be comics on the couch. I was in charge of the fire, so every now and then I'd throw on a block of timber or a sod of turf and give the bellows a turn. The bellows, or 'bellis', as everybody called it, was like a bicycle wheel with a protruding handle. By taking the handle and turning the big wheel, a smaller wheel connected to the big one by a bicycle tyre would rotate vigorously, generate a good sturdy draught beneath the floor of the fireplace and whoosh the fire back into a flurry of sparks and flames. From behind the newspaper would come the order to curb my enthusiasm. 'Go aisey or you'll burn us out of house and home.'

'The couch' was actually the back seat of a scrapped Morris Minor, bolted to a large block of timber to raise the whole contraption to knee height. The plush springs added to the fun of the experience. If a small boy launched himself carelessly onto the couch, the car springs' recoil would project him, without pity, back to the hard flagstone floor whence he came.

'That's life for you,' Johnny would note, without looking up from his newspaper. 'If you don't look before you leap, you'll end up sitting on your backside feeling sorry for yourself.'

ooo

Apart from sharing a name, we shared a love of comics, and Johnny was always delighted when I would bring a bundle of used ones down from the city. Once the house was settled, Johnny would swap a Trigger bar for one of my comics. He could have just given me the Trigger bar, but I think he was teaching me how to bargain. I wouldn't be much of a farmer if I just sold a cow for the first price I was offered.

'What's Terrible Dan up to this week?' he'd enquire.

'It's Desperate Dan!' I'd correct him.

'You're right, it *is* desperate. But my name isn't Dan.'

'You say that every week, Johnny,' I sighed. 'I was thinking ...'

'Didn't I warn you about thinking? 'Tis the source of all trouble.'

'I know, Johnny, but anyway ... Dennis the Menace is in a donkey derby here and I was thinking ... Deirdre is like lightning and I'm after getting very good as a jockey, I'd say.'

He laughed and snorted. 'Go on.'

'Well, I was thinking ... is there any donkey derby that we could enter?'

'Oh, there is.'

'A donkey derby?'

'Yes.'

'Where?'

'Here.'

'Here?'

'Well, near here.'

'Near here? Where near here?'

'Oh, I'm not sure exactly where it's on this year, but I'll check.'

'Will it be on a school day or can we go in for it?'

'Sure, I don't know. I'll have to enquire. That'll do now. Put away the comics and go out and make your pooley before we hit the hay.'

'I'll be all right.'

'Sure, how could you be all right? You haven't gone out all night and you'll never go the whole night without soaking yourself in the bed.'

'I'll wait till the morning altogether.'

'Is it scared of the dark you are?'

No reply.

'Ah sure, you'll have to get over that too. What kind of man will you make if you're scared of the dark and wetting the bed? I mean, what woman would marry a man who's scared of the dark and wets the bed? Huh? Erra, go out now and make your pooley.'

As I lifted the latch, Mick cocked an ear, and as soon as I gave him the nod he was out the door in a flash and into the high grass, sniffing around to make his own business. Scared to look behind me, I stood as close as possible to the faint glow from the tiny kitchen window. I fumbled in my corduroys and waited. Nothing.

What kind of man will I be? I wondered. *I'll never get a wife. Johnny hasn't a wife. I could be like Johnny and live on my own. But not if I'm still scared of the dark. How do you get not afraid of the dark? Is it the same way as small boys like me eventually get a taste for the beer?*

Mick had gone off on one of his rambles, but he came back when I called him. Some nights when you'd let him out to do his business, he'd clear off. But he'd always be outside the cottage door in the morning.

There was only one bedroom and one bed in Lackenroe, but there was a storeroom with no window, so Johnny had turned it into a makeshift bedroom for me. He got an old iron-framed bed from someone and put an orange box beside it as a bedside locker. Above my head was a dusty shelf holding tins of half-used paint and a big jam jar with old paint brushes that smelled of turpentine. Half a ton of spuds was heaped against the wall at the end of my bed and the unplastered walls had a spider in every nook and a daddy-long-legs in every cranny.

On the first night I stayed there I couldn't sleep. Eventually, I crept barefoot across the cold flagstones of the darkened kitchen and stood outside Johnny's bedroom. I couldn't think of any other solution other than knocking on it. From inside, I could first hear Mick growl and then Johnny's voice.

'Bruh ... hello? Is that yourself?'

'I'm scared. Can I come in?'

'What? Jesus, will you go back to bed for yourself?' was the sleepy reply from within.

'I can't, I'm scared. I can't sleep on my own. Can I come in there?'

'Jesus Christ, go on so,' he groaned. 'Climb in there beside me and keep quiet.'

I did and within seconds Johnny was sound asleep again. I was awake until dawn came in the window, but at least there were three of us in the room. I must have nodded off then, because when I woke, Johnny was gone, the cows had been milked and the bed was drenched. I tried to dry it with newspapers and I opened the window, but I think Johnny already knew. I was scared he was going to give out to me when he got back from work, but he didn't. He just asked, 'How are the men?' and then disappeared into the bedroom for ages.

When he came out, he had the sheets in a bag and he brought them out to the boot of the car and drove off. When he returned to the cottage, he announced that he had bought a Gateaux Swiss Roll for after dinner. That was our favourite cake.

'Will I put on the spuds?'

'Do,' he said, 'and you can take Mick down to the room with you tonight for a bit of company.'

I knew then that Johnny loved me.

Johnny's snoring would wake the dead, but from then on it was the donkey derby that was keeping me awake. *Imagine if I won! I will have to decide between Rosie and Deirdre, though, and I will really have to come down every Saturday to train, train, train.*

I read the cardboard boxes Johnny kept on top of the wardrobe with all the animal medicines: 'Cheno Unction for Mastitis – A Quare Name But Great Stuff!', 'Palm Grove Ice Cream', 'Jaffa Oranges – Produce of Israel'. *That's where God's from*, I thought to myself. *They probably have brilliant camel races there. I could make friends with the other jockeys and tell them all about donkey derbies in Ireland. I'd have to get a camel with two humps, though, so that I wouldn't fall off.*

Tom the Traveller

I was a regular in Lackenroe that summer and became a dab hand at milking cows, thinning and weeding vegetables, and all the rest of it. But no matter how excited I'd get about going to Lackenroe, once I'd arrive, I'd be bored. There was nobody to play with. It was a bit like Christmas – you'd spend the whole year looking forward to it, but once it came and you got the toys, that was it. All your friends had to stay in their own houses and it got dark early.

Johnny said it was the same with adults. 'Dinnie Buckley's younger brother, Boring Buckley, got married years ago. Himself and herself got all excited about going on their honeymoon. They were telling everyone about it and how they would be flying with Aer Lingus, if you don't mind. They said they'd be staying in a French hotel. There's posh! Going to France and staying in a French hotel and all. But as soon as they got to Lourdes, the boredom set in and they hated it. They had no French, so they had no one to talk to, only themselves. Then the talking stopped and that was the end of it. Honeymoon over. So y'see, the reason you're bored is because you're boring.'

'What?'

'The reason you're bored is because you're boring.'

'How d'ya mean?' I asked.

'Well, I mean, if you were a gas man, you wouldn't be bored, would you?'

'I s'pose not.'

'Well, take yourself off for a walk there for yourself. Here's a tanner for the shop. Go across the fields and keep off the road and bring Mick with you.'

'OK, thanks,' I said, but inside I was sighing with the boredom.

The Sugarloaf shop was about twenty minutes away, across the fields, towards Knockraha. There was only one spot where you came out onto the road, so I'd put the lead on Mick there and listen for the furthest-away sound to make sure there wasn't any traffic. When all of my senses assured me it was safe to cross, I did so, gingerly and totally in the moment.

If there was no one around, I'd sit on the windowsill of the Sugarloaf and eat my cone. The gobstopper would stay in my pants pocket until comics time later. Mick would always get the 'baby cone', which I made by breaking off the very bottom of the wafer cone and scooping a small blob of the whipped ice cream on top.

Invariably, the return journey to the cottage was slower as I surrendered to nature's charms. *Dordán na mbeach*, that sonorous humming of bees that ran all along the hedgerow, is a very particular sound. Not quite a buzz, more like a low hum that would sometimes shift tone like the drones on a set of uilleann pipes.

Hypnotised by the buzzing of bees and birdsong, I stepped through the boredom portal into a world of contentment where I could be distracted by life's insignificances – the great unnoticed. I could get five minutes following a bumblebee from flower to flower, stuffing yellow pollen into his back pockets. I wondered if his furry Kilkenny jumper felt fuzzy like the velvet curtains in our sitting room. Sometimes, Mick and myself would fall asleep in the heat of a haycock out in the meadow. The hay was dry and warm and sweet-smelling like a woman's cardigan. Other times, I'd lie on my back and look up at the sky, wondering what was wrong with me and if God was trying to send me a message through the shapes of the clouds. Not really – they were mostly cloud-shaped, with the occasional bad map of Ireland or some kind of animal's head making an appearance.

On a few occasions, a single ray of bright sunshine pierced a cloud and pointed, like a bullet-beam, down to Earth, as if to say, 'YOU! YOU SHALL GIVE UP THY EARTHLY GOODS AND FOLLOW ME!' However, a sunbeam never made landfall in the field

I was in, so maybe it was some other fella with a vocation getting the calling.

One day in the meadow, I was thinking about the picture of the Sacred Heart on the kitchen wall at home. Spud Murphy once told me that Jesus had been shot for Ireland and that he was holding his guts in his hands, but my mother said he was showing us his heart to let us know he loved us and, no matter what we had done, he would forgive us. You could see the forgiveness in his eyes. It was like he was saying, 'Don't mind the shirt off me back, I'd give you the heart right out of me body.'

I was starting to agree with Jesus. You have to forgive people. I mean, Mam had forgiven the drunk man in the shop who was roaring and cursing at her. I remembered her saying that he was some poor woman's baby once. Mick, too, would have got the electric chair below in the dogs' home if the Christian Brother he dragged off the bicycle hadn't forgiven him. Mick got a second chance. Johnny gave me a second chance after I wet the bed. If I was going to be a priest, I'd have to forgive a whole queue of people every night at Confession and give them all a second chance. Even the Brother in school I wanted to murder with a big rock would have to be forgiven if I wanted to be like Jesus. If the Sacred Heart could forgive him, maybe I should too. Anyway, Mick had already gotten back at the Christian Brothers by dragging a good few of them off their bicycles, so we were quits.

There were few pubs, or kids, around Glounthaune. Some older boys would gather outside the Sugarloaf and sit on the windowsill of the shop. It stayed open until the pub closed, so lads and moths would gather in the glow of the shop window until the lights went off. Then everyone went home. The lads never went into the pub. They weren't allowed.

I often watched them from the car while I was waiting for Johnny to come out of the shop with the messages. They just stood outside the shop all night, mocking each other. Sometimes, if a girl was sent down to the shop by her mam, they'd mock her once she was gone in. They weren't brave enough to mock her to her face, so when she'd come out again, they'd all go quiet, until one of them would mumble something as she walked past. Then they'd all start skitting and the girl would know that they were mocking her. I hated that, but then I remembered how we all teased Click-Clack Charlie about his stutter on the way home from school. It's strange how much fun you can get from mocking someone.

These were the kinds of things I used to think about when there was no one around and I could talk to myself in my own head. Sometimes, I'd talk out loud to the animals, especially Mick, Rosie and

Teresa McGonagle. They were no craic, but they were great listeners.

ooo

Some nights, to get a break from all my talking, Johnny would take me over to Crowley's. I knew the way across the fields and some days I would just head there myself.

Tadgh and Norah Crowley lived in a rambling house. Not the kind of 'rambling house' as defined in an auctioneer's blurb, with servants' quarters and a Victorian orangery. No, Crowley's was a two-bedroom cottage, but it was well known as a 'rambling house' in the traditional sense – a tradition that thrived in a place and time before television, comedy clubs and late bars. Neighbours would ramble in unannounced and the evening would take on a life of its own. The shy ones would make for an inconspicuous perch where they could watch proceedings.

Teaghlach lán-Ghaelach ab ea é, freisin. Crowley's was also an Irish-speaking household. They spoke Gaeilge na Mumhan, that beautiful dialect of Irish found amongst the Irish-speakers of Munster – in this case, Múscraí in mid-Cork, where they were born. However, if required, the hosts would generously switch gears to English to meet the company. Their collie, Prince, also spoke Irish. Not just the commands of '*suigh síos*', '*stad*' and '*amach leat*' (sit down, stop, out with you), he also knew full well what '*dinnéar*', '*madra*' and '*leaba*' (dinner, dog, bed) meant.

Tadgh and Norah were in their early eighties and partially sighted, but both had a keen ear. Norah for words – she never forgot a name or a story – and Tadgh for a melody. He could play a new tune on his fiddle after just one hearing. He often played into the night and never seemed to notice the sticky white powder that attached itself to the lap of his trousers as the rosin fell from his bow. 'Rosin the Bow' was his nickname, but you would never call him that to his face. Not because he was cross. The opposite. Because he was so gentle and kind that you wouldn't want to hurt his feelings. In fact, 'Rosin the Bow' was more of a pet name than a nickname, if that makes sense.

There were three framed pictures on display in the house and Jesus was in the middle. I liked him a lot. His eyes looked very caring. You couldn't look Patrick Pearse in the eye, however. Himself and John F. Kennedy were both in profile only, looking at Jesus from their places on the wall. It was a bit like the good thief and the bad thief on either side of Jesus at the crucifixion. It was clear to me that Patrick Pearse was cross. Mrs Crowley used to say that JFK's white teeth were a sure sign that the Kennedys had done well for themselves in America.

It never struck me as odd that the only pictures in the house were of men who were assassinated. All three of them had stood up for the poor people and got murdered for their troubles. They were setting a very high standard for the rest of us. As there was no television or other kids to play with, I looked at those pictures a lot, and Jesus was definitely my favourite.

I would sit on the settle bench. I loved that my feet didn't reach the ground; instead my legeens swung back and forth to the tunes until the music stopped and I switched over to the hypnotic rhythm of the pendulum in the old clock as some storyteller whispered their tale.

The rhythms of that country kitchen led me, once again, through the boredom portal into a spacious place. Even the droning of the old people was hypnotic. Like the humming of bees, their soft pastoral tones and broad vowels called me to sleep. Sometimes Norah would lay a folded blanket over me and whisper, 'Musha, *codladh sámh, a stór*' (sleep well, my dear).

The Rosary, too, would hypnotise me. I would resist the repetitive beat of the Our Father, ten Hail Marys and a Glory Be until the rhythm overcame me like a wave outrunning a boat in their race to shore. And then ... surrender.

One evening my teenage cousin Denis was up at Crowley's when the Rosary struck up, and for pure mischief, he decided to set an endurance test for the faithful, so when he got to the tenth and final Hail Mary ... he just kept going. The old people who did their counting on their rosary beads were starting to raise an eyebrow. We waited for the Glory Be that signals the end of the decade, but Denis kept praying and, of course, you cannot interrupt the devout at prayer. You can cough, however, so Norah gave a few deliberate 'Ahem-hems' in an attempt to get Denis's attention and rein him in. The prayers continued like a runaway train and the increasingly laboured responses of the congregation went unheeded. Each time Denis started a new 'Hail Mary, full of grace ...' a groan ran through the room. I tried to keep in a snicker, but it came out as a whistle through my nose. Denis was starting his twenty-eighth Hail Mary when Pat Finnegan finally erupted.

'Ah, for the love of Jesus Christ, willyu shtop, you little hure?!'

He did.

ooo

For much of the day, the Crowleys' front door was left on the latch and the kettle was left on the boil in case someone might call.

One morning in early January, I found myself on my usual perch, watching the *bean a' tí* making a brown cake using the rhythm method. Several cupfuls of wholemeal brown flour, a couple of cupfuls of white flour, a fist of oat flakes when she had them, a small spoonful of bread soda, a good sup of buttermilk, a pinch of salt and a large dollop of experience. She could continue a conversation without stopping to measure ingredients. In that regard, every single loaf she made was entirely unique.

This morning's mantra was a rhythmic *olagón*ing about the bad weather. Norah's monologue set the tempo for the up–down motion of the big, long, watery snot that dangled from her nostril. Transfixed by its elasticity, I wondered to myself if, maybe, the other nostril was blocked. I stared incredulously as the icicle stretched just short of breaking point, a full two inches from her nose tip, and then straight back up again when she inhaled.

If she sneezes ... I thought.

The rhythm of the work was broken when a knock came to the door. The man behind the knock was known as 'Tom the Traveller', a big, hulking man. Tom was one of a number of people who didn't need to knock on the door, but he always did. He was shy and would often speak through his fingers as he rubbed his face. Prince recognised the knock and merely raised one ear, without moving.

Tom greeted both house and household with his customary blessing: '*Dia anseo isteach*' (God be with all here).

'*Fáilte, a Thomáis. Tar isteach as an drochaimsir sin,*' (Welcome, Tom. Come in out of that bad weather) replied Norah, beckoning him towards the open fire.

Apart from the rosary beads and the holy pictures he'd sell you for a few pence, Tom was the bringer of news. Because he walked the roads and was welcome everywhere he went, Tom knew better than most what was going on. Some people called him 'The News of the World' after the English newspaper.

'*Aon trácht ar Danny Maidhc?*' (Any word on Danny Mike?) the *bean a' tí* enquired.

'Erra, he's poor. Gone up to bed to die, I believe. The boys are all coming home from Boston, so I expect he hasn't long now, poor man.'

Tom was no liar, but his timing could be out. Once, when he said that old Con Downey was dead, he was out by almost a year. Indeed, Con had been anointed by the priest, but wasn't quite ready to throw in the towel and spent the last few months of his life with a collection of Mass cards for the repose of his soul beside him on the bedside locker.

On this occasion, Tom's news and forecast were deadly accurate. I was told to 'shove up on the forrum' and make room for him.

'Give d'oul bellis a twirl and redden the fire,' added Norah.

My favourite job. A few turns of the bellows and the embers whooshed back to life.

My attention switched from the icicle on Norah's nose to the curtain of steam now rising from the sodden shoulders of Tom's greatcoat. And his coat was great. It was made of heavy wool and had a huge thick collar. Expensive when it was new, there was now a button or two missing, but he kept it tied with a length of twine threaded through the belt loops. Someone said Tom once got a few days' work from a farmer during fine spring weather, and he left the coat he used to wear back then hanging on a nail in the farmer's shed for the few sunny days. But when the hailstones returned, Tom went back to retrieve his coat only to discover that a wren had built her nest in the pocket. There was nothing for it but to put on the coat, finish his jobs and hang it up again that evening for the wren to get on with her own business, and she did. When Tom finished up the work, the farmer's wife made him a gift of one of her husband's unwanted old coats rather than displace the entire wren family. The gesture was a win-win-win for all involved.

That fine coat was now drying in front of the fire as the conversation continued. I could see Tom had also become transfixed by the miracle of Mrs Crowley's nose.

Unannounced, as befits the man of the house, the *fear a' tí* lifted the latch and kicked off one of his boots using the other. Tadgh had been out rattling a bucket for the calves, but with another shower imminent, he withdrew to the warmth of home.

He greeted all present and listened intently to Tom's news bulletin. Because the visit was usually a short one, Tadgh stirred himself and enquired, '*Bhuel, a Thomáis, bhfuil tú chun bóthair?*' (Well, Tom, are you for the road?)

With a discreet nod in Norah's direction, Tom replied, '*Braitheann sé má thitfidh an cith.*' (It depends on if the shower will fall.)

'*Ceart go leor,*' (Fair enough) said Tadgh.

I think it may have gone over Norah's head, but old Mr Crowley and myself both understood full well what Tom was actually saying. Effectively, 'If she gets the brown cake into the oven before the icicle plops into the dough, I'll stay for the grub. But if the shower falls ... I'm gone!'

A nod is as good as a wink to a blind man, you might say.

Mrs Manley

Deirdre was probably faster than Rosie, but she was half mad. Rosie was a bit older, but at least she'd stand for me as I harnessed her to the cart. Bridle, blinkers and bit to make sure she knew which direction the boy at the other end of the reins wanted her to go. I'd lift the old wooden collar around her neck, ensuring the padding was comfortable for her, and check that the bit in her mouth wasn't too tight. Then I'd try to get her to reverse into position so I could tackle her to the cart. But she was immovable, literally. Once or twice she inadvertently stood on my toe as I tackled her and there was no shifting her. Talking gently or roaring, 'Get off my bloody foot!' seemed to go straight in one furry ear, across the empty cavity of her skull and out the furry ear on the other side. She just looked straight ahead, stoically. Johnny was right. There is no talking to donkeys.

Bodhar Uí Laoighre was a beggarman long ago who would show up on Fair Days back west-along. 'Bodhar Uí Laoighre' means 'Deaf O'Leary', because he had a sign around his neck with 'Deaf from Birth' scrawled on it. He'd sit in the square and beg for coppers.

One day, some toff in a top hat decided to test him. 'My good man, I would like to give you some money for your troubles. However, I have no change, just a pound note.'

'Shur, I'll change it for you, sir,' says O'Leary, reaching into his pocket.

All donkeys have a touch of the old Bodhar Uí Laoighre in them. They'll only hear what they want to hear.

However, Mrs Manley, who lived nearby, had a great way with donkeys, or 'dunkeys', as she called them.

'Hould her steady there now and let me talk to her,' she'd say, handing me the reins. 'Erra, Rosie, what's wrong with you at all, pet, hah? Are the men driving you quare, hah? I don't blame you one bit, girl ... dem two Johnnies would drive any woman clane off her game.'

Leaning her own shoulder back into the donkey's chest, she'd encourage Rosie into reverse. 'Good girl, c'mon now, heck up, just one shtep, heck up. That's the job. You're the best dunkey in the whole of Cork.'

I loved Mrs Manley. She smelt of damp turf and stale Woodbines and lived across the fields in a moss-covered cottage on a half-acre. She always wore a headscarf knotted below her chin and a pair of wellingtons turned down at the knee. I loved the way she'd use a goose wing to move the dust around the house. But more than anything, I loved the way she treated me as a friend, not just some child. She'd tell me private stuff and things about the neighbours. Once when I got stung on the back of the neck by a wasp, she ran all the way back to her own house to get Dettol, even though she was old and 'crippled with de hip'.

Mrs Manley told me she was born in 1907 and had no children. I loved the way she said 'guverment' and 'the divil fire 'em anyway!' I often wondered what that meant. At first I thought 'the divil fire 'em' might mean that she hoped the devil would sack them from their jobs. It was only later that I realised she was actually invoking Satan to heap reddened coals on top of them. A lot of people used to say that about politicians and the Kerry footballers and the Tipperary hurlers too.

One morning in the milking stall, she roared, 'The curse of Christ down on top of you anyway,' when Teresa McGonagle kicked over a bucket of milk.

'No point crying over spilt milk, Mrs Manley,' said I, bravely.

She once caught me robbing one of her fags and trying to smoke it out in the cow shed. 'Yerra, they won't do you much harm, but you'll stay small, mind you. You won't grow. Doctor Browne told me that years ago. Didn't Dan Deasy below in the Sugarloaf give 'em up when he re-married and he swelled back up to a frightening size altogether? He went back on the Mars Bars, and they're complete demons altogether. Taytos and Mars Bars till he nearly burst! So, if you don't mind being small, shmoke away, let you. You'll come to no harm.'

One time, Dr Browne gave her a lift in his pride and joy, a brand-new Ford Zephyr, complete with built-in radio and a pop-out cigarette lighter set into its walnut dashboard. Without asking, Mrs Manley rummaged for her five-pack of Woodbines and took out a topper to re-light it. Rummaging for matches, she leaned over towards the driver, all elbows and grunting with the hip.

'What's wrong with you?' he snapped.

'Well, 'tisn't fleas, I'm only trying to find my matches.'

'Don't mind your ould matches,' he scoffed. 'Wait till you see this!'

With an experienced finger, he inserted the lighter on the dashboard.

'Wait a minute now,' he instructed, 'give it a chance.'

And sure enough, once reddened, it automatically ejected from the hole. Mrs Manley recoiled in surprise.

'Now,' he announced proudly, 'take a light offa that!'

Wide-eyed, Mrs Manley took the lighter by the black Bakelite handle and peered into the reddened core. 'Jaysus Chrisht, but isn't that the dandiest little invention ever?' was her verdict. She stuck the Woodbine butt between her pursed lips and sucked, as she brought the glowing lighter perilously close to her nose hair.

Dr Browne took it all in, admiring his new toy as though it were part of the NASA mission to the moon, with the capsule docking perfectly. *We have ignition*, he probably thought.

As Mrs Manley exhaled a good lungful of blue smoke, she flicked her wrist as though quenching a match in her hand and, without missing a beat of that age-old ritual, she flung the lighter out the open window. The driver was speechless.

Come daylight, Dr Browne was back to the scene of the crime with no success. Every Sunday, he could be seen poking amongst the brambles, looking for his lighter. Some people said the hole in his walnut dashboard was the eventual killing of him.

Whatever about Mrs Manley's shortcomings with modern transport, she was a dinger with the old ones: donkeys. She had me back on my two-raw-eggs-in-a-half-cup-of-milk routine in preparation for the derby. Twice a day, I'd get Rosie's attention with a carrot or an apple up my sleeve and tackle her, without the cart, for training. For the most part, training was about keeping the donkey going and keeping myself on board at the same time. We trained in the middle of the day, when the farm work stopped for the Angelus, a bite of grub and for Johnny to listen to the news on Radio Éireann.

When Charles Mitchel was calling out the news, Johnny, just like my dad, kept saying 'Whisht!' and 'Shhh!', even though I hadn't said a word. Even Mick looked confused. I think Johnny only said 'Whisht' and 'Shhh' because he couldn't believe his ears. I remember one day hearing Charles Mitchel saying that Buzz Aldrin was walking on the moon and had left a message up there from Eamon de Valera, our president, asking God for peace and happiness down here on Earth. Another day Charles said that the ha'penny and farthing would be gone soon because we were getting new money and there would be 100 pennies in the pound, not 240 anymore. There was always some excitement back then. Another time, Charles said that the other crowd above in Belfast had come down to Dublin and set off a bomb in RTÉ. When I saw Mrs Manley on the passage later that day, I told her about 'd'other crowd from the North' and she said, 'The divil fire 'em anyway!'

Later in the day, after the Angelus, news and grub at six o'clock, I'd tackle the donkey again and flake around the top field, which was the biggest and it had a good slope for getting Rosie fit for any unexpected gradient on the course. In my head, and sometimes out loud, if no one could hear me, I'd vocalise Michael O'Hehir's commentary on the race:

'And as they turn for home, it's Arkle, ridden by Pat Taaffe, out in front by two lengths, but Rosie with young John Creedon on board is staying the pace. They're into the final furlong and, despite a right good flakin' from her rider, Gold Cup winner Arkle seems to be losing ground to the newcomer from Cork. And as they cross the line it's the donkey who shades it. Yes! Yes! It's Rosie by a nose.'

The reality was, however, that I kept falling off. There was no saddle and, despite Johnny roaring advice like 'Squeeze in your legs' or 'Hould her mane AND the reins' or 'Ah, for Christ's sake', I'd still fall off. If she started that tippy-toe trotting that donkeys do, the bumping would knock me off. If she took off suddenly at the start, I'd recoil and roll off backwards. If she decided to put her head down, I'd roll off the front. Johnny told me I wouldn't be disqualified for falling off, once I got back up again and crossed the finishing line on board the donkey. So at least I could say I finished the race, even if the better lads took first, second and third.

Once, when trying to remount, I threw myself up on the moving donkey's back and went straight over the other side and landed with a thump. Mrs Manley started laughing. I got in a right huff and didn't speak to her until the following day.

When Johnny was working, Mrs Manley would often come up to milk the cows. It was tough going on a cold morning, but I'd have the three cows in their stalls and a spancel on Teresa McGonagle before Mrs Manley arrived. We wouldn't be long warming up, sitting there on our three-legged stools, up to our shins in straw, heads pressed against the warm side of a cow. She would milk the two big ones and I'd work away, the best I could, on the Blue Cow, until Mrs Manley was ready to finish her off. Sometimes, for mischief, she'd squirt a long stream of warm milk straight from the cow's pap and hit me or Mick on the back of the head. She had a deadly aim and you'd never see it coming. 'I'm like the one-eyed gunner,' she'd laugh. I tried the same on her once but got her right in the face. She leapt up and roared, 'Christ, you've blinded me, you hure!'

If the sows were farrowing, they always seemed to do it at night, and because Johnny had work in the morning, Mrs Manley, Mick and myself became the midwives. A farrowing crate would take centre stage, and a generous few fistfuls of dry, shiny, butter-coloured straw would be tossed liberally on the eight-foot by four-foot base of the crate. Mrs Manley and myself would lure the sow into the farrowing crate with a bucket of warm, wet pig ration, and then we would offer the expectant mother a bucket of bran to 'bring her on'. An infrared bulb swung from a cable that was draped along a cobweb-covered roof beam. That was plugged into a plugboard that in turn was plugged into an old two-pin socket beside the Sacred Heart light in the kitchen in the house. It provided the required glow of warmth for the new arrivals and cast a cosy red hue on the proceedings.

Henrietta the hen, sensing action, arrived into the warmth of the infrared bulb in the farrowing shed, away from the darkness and the risks posed by the nocturnal opportunism of Mister Fox. Mrs Manley, arms folded across her belly, hunched forward on her three-legged milking stool and raised the Tilley lamp to see better. She spotted Henrietta and declared, 'Yerra, look who's in. I tell you, eggs are grand, but to hell with poverty, we'll kill the hen.'

Now, I'm not sure you could say that a hen has an actual face, but I could have sworn there was a startled look in Henrietta's beady little eyes as she cock-stepped herself back out the door of the shed and slipped away into the night. She'd rather face a hungry fox than a hungry Mrs Manley any day or night.

With the labour ward to ourselves again, Mrs Manley squinted towards the business end of the sow and continued her commentary. 'That's number fourteen now. Did you know a sow would eat her own young?'

'Holy God!' said I.

Mick was sniffing around the newly born bonhams, nuzzling any strays back into the heat of the crate and onto the comfort of their mother's distended teat.

Amused at Mick's display of maternal instinct, Mrs Manley chuckled, 'Erra, poor ole Mickeen. You're mad for the babies, aren't you? Hah?' she asked, as she scratched him under the chin. 'You are,' she agreed with herself, 'you're shtone mad for the babies, you poor ole craythur. And you can't have no babies, hah? You couldn't even lay an oul' egg! Heh heh.' She cackled away to herself, pleased at her own humour and safe in the expectation that I wouldn't understand. I laughed too, thinking of Mick laying an egg.

The delivery would go on late into the night. Mrs Manley was the midwife, Mick was the babysitter, and I'd keep count. A litter of 18 or 20 bonhams wasn't unusual and I'd try to stay awake to tell Johnny the tally when he woke for work.

On Sunday night I'd be sorry to leave the baby pigs and Mick and Mrs Manley behind, but Johnny would have to get me back to the city for school.

Saints, Sinners and Santy

My heart sank as Johnny's Morris Minor approached the darkness on the edge of town.

Dunkettle roundabout, the revolving door that sorted traffic from the east, discharged us at the new industrial estate at Tivoli Docks. Yellow street lights illuminated footpaths where nobody ever walked, and factories released steam into the night sky.

With the anxiety of an astronaut on re-entry, I braced myself for my return. Yeah, there'd be new comics in the shop and I'd see my sisters and brothers again, but after the spaciousness of the meadows and the silence of aloneness, I'd have to face the G-force of the city centre, school, the relentless shop bell and the words I had grown to hate: 'John! You're wanted!'

I shared my mother's longing for the countryside. She was always in good form when reminiscing about Adrigole and her father's horse and the collie and the corncrake and the primroses. She loved primroses.

By comparison, life in the city promised prosperity and a university education for her children, but the work was relentless. Mam would complain about 'the menagerie', as she called it – the constantly evolving assortment of dogs, cats, guinea pigs, budgies and any other animal with that 'shu'gawd helpus' look. We even had a bantam hen and cock out in the backyard. Himself was eventually sent west because his body clock was totally out of sync with the rest of the neighbours. My dad used to call the house '*Rus in urbe*'. He said it was Latin for 'countryside in the city'. He was right.

On Saturday mornings, if Johnny hadn't already collected me, my mother would call us at around six to see the rodeo. Three or four of us younger ones would wait in the darkened shop, keeping watch through the window for the first sign of it. Standing on chairs, our little cowboy hats peeped over the fruit display at a street, empty apart from a few gulls squabbling over last night's chip wrappers. Then, like distant thunder or the early-warning shudder of an earthquake, a low rumble would roll in from the Blackpool end of Leitrim Street and put the gulls in a flap. *They're on the way!*

Suddenly, a panic-stricken little boy with a stick would enter stage right, running to take up his position across the street at the open gate of the Munster Hotel. Within seconds another little boy in wellies and a flat cap would screech to a halt outside our shop window, arms and legs spread to block the escape route down Devonshire Street. More tiny drovers would arrive and overlap their amigos to block off the small lane, the big lane, Bridge Street and every side street and alley all the way to the docks.

Then would come the thunderous drum roll of hooves, horns, hups and hahs as hundreds of confused cattle of every variety stampeded up our street. With bulging wild eyes and flared nostrils, they skittered in the manure of the front-runners. One of them would surely burst through the glass and onto our fruit display, I thought.

The little drovers took off again and, using shortcuts, outflanked the cattle to take up their next positions along the route that led all the way to the ramp of the boat waiting at Penrose Quay to take them away to England and their destiny.

ooo

Shortly afterwards, the 'Shop Open' sign was turned to face the world again and the procession of humans began. Most of them would stay on their own side of the counter, but others would sail in behind it and into the kitchen for a visit.

Everyone will have an opinion on the merits, or otherwise, of the unannounced visitor. Ireland, we're led to believe, is the Land of a Hundred Thousand Welcomes, the *céad míle fáilte*. The Celtic predilection for hospitality was underlined by the monastic system that was established here in the

400s. According to the Rule of Benedict, the stranger is to be welcomed as though it were Christ himself at the door. However, when the door swings open and the householder declares 'Christ!', it's not necessarily a declaration of welcome. The unannounced visitor is a pest.

Y'see, there's an etiquette around visiting. The second-most important rule is to always arrive on time. But the most important rule is to leave on time. Nuns had a papal dispensation from this rule, particularly if they were back from the Missions. They had all day.

In fairness, their stories about Africa and the jungle were usually very good, but the most important thing about a visiting nun was the Cinderella rule. You had to make sure that she was gone before the clock struck 12, because if you don't have a nun out of the house by midday, the bells will ring out the Angelus and then you're rightly scuppered. She'll start with 'The Angel of the Lord declared unto Mary ...' then look at your blank expression for the response. Something like 'And she was conceived by the fruit of the womb' is close, but not good enough. You simply had to get them out of the house before the bell tolled at midday.

Luckily, another member of the religious who regularly visited our shop never obeyed the twice-a-day-Angelus rule. Mind you, he never obeyed the two golden rules of visiting either. Fr Casey would arrive unannounced and prop up our shop counter telling endless stories about his time as a missionary, as my mother tried to serve customers around him.

Fr Casey was elderly and could be best described as a 'bachelor' priest. He clearly needed a wife or a housekeeper or someone to keep a *smacht* on him, but he had nobody.

His childhood had been spent labouring on the family farm on the side of a steep mountain in Kerry. His father, his older brother and himself did all the pullin' and draggin' in all kinds of weather, while his mother and younger sister did all the housework. It was just the way it was.

Once, when I was about seven years old and considering religious life myself, I sought his advice. I asked him why he had decided to become a priest and how did he know he had a vocation.

He thought for a moment and said, 'Eh ... yerra, I dunno. I suppose, I was the second eldest ... and the next one down was a girl. It was a mother's vocation really, I suppose.'

Fr Casey now lived in a huge 12-bedroom presbytery with three other retired priests. His black suit could have badly done with a dry-clean. The shoulders and lapels were covered in dandruff and the fabric was so old and worn that you could see your face in the shine. The suit was so stretched and baggy, 'twas said you could hatch a goose in the seat of his trousers. I once saw the same gravy stain on the front of his cardigan for nearly a year. Furthermore, he chain-smoked Gold Flake cigarettes and only ate when he remembered.

However, Fr Casey had a heart of gold and was as innocent as the driven snow. He looked after older priests. Fr Con had taken to the bed and refused to get up.

'He passes his time *olagón*ing,' Fr Casey told us. 'The poor craythur spends most of the day saying, "I haven't much time left. I'm away to bed to die. I'm of no use to anyone anymore." I give him the same answer every time. I say, "Erra, I dunno. I mean, didn't Our Blessed Lord himself do some of his finest work in the last few days before he died?" That quietens him and his complaining.'

Fr Casey would spend hours standing at my mother's shop counter recalling 'the good ole days, back west-along in Kerry' or his many foreign adventures on the Missions, all peppered with those Latin expressions that permeated the everyday conversations of those who grew up in the age of the Latin Mass. I remember my mother behind the counter, leaning on the Cadbury's stand, arms folded with her chin resting on her open palm.

'Oh Christ, I loved Nye-geer-ah,' he'd enthuse. I loved the way he pronounced Nigeria. It reminded me of the way old cowboys would say 'Virginny' when speaking of Virginia. 'Oh Christ, they were the dandiest people you could meet. We were living in the parochial house in Iva Valley in Enugu. We worked hard and I loved it, man.' He called everyone 'man', even my mother.

'Christ, we'd be up at six o'clock in the morning and we'd have to travel for up to four hours in the back of an oul' truck, up into the mountains. You'd have to keep your head down on the way up and the way back.'

'Branches?'

'Christ no, blow darts. If the lads with the blow pipes spotted you, Christ, you'd get it, man. One touch of one of them and you'd be paralysed. You'd be rightly wasting your time sending to Lagos for an ambulance.'

My mother and myself glanced at each other, shocked that someone would try to kill a priest.

'But once we got safely up to the clinic, we'd give them whatever had come out from Ireland: buckets, hoes, medicines, stuff for the women, toys for the children and a few copies of the Igbo catechism for those who had any interest. To be honest, there wasn't much we could teach those people about faith, hope and charity.

'I'd say Mass and Sister Bernadette would fire a few injections into them and we'd be gone again before dark lest we had to face the lads with the darts on the way back down. Sister Bernadette used often say, "I have to get the needle into them before the other crowd get the darts into us." And I'd always say, "Good medicine over bad, Sister."

'If them lads didn't get you, the mosquitos would. Oh, you could be killed shtone dead by a shting from one of dem ladeens, God blasht 'em. Sure, isn't that why the Brits invented the gin and tonic, man. There's quinine in the tonic. That stops the malaria. The Brits were the boys who ruled the world, so they knew a thing or two about batin' the mozzies at their own game. That's why we'd have a gin and tonic when we'd get back to base.

'Christ, we'd be exhausted, man, but we'd always have d'oul gin and tonic, a bite of grub, then I'd read my breviary, say my prayers and be up again at five in the morning. It was tough going but we loved the people, man.'

The story paused momentarily as Fr Casey lit a fresh cigarette off the last and my mother tutted a tut of concern rather than disapproval.

'You'll have to start looking after yourself, Father.'

'Ah, sure d'oul fags are my only vice. I'm flying it now, but when I got called back to Ireland, I was sick as a dog, very bad. I couldn't sleep. The lads above said, "That's the jet lag, Casey," but no, I had it for months ... and desperate sweating and nightmares.

'The doctor tried all kinds of tests, but he couldn't crack it. He asked me, "What changes have you made in your lifestyle since you got back from Africa? Have you changed anything?"

'"Lifeshtyle? I dunno," says I. "I s'pose I'd be eating more spuds and less rice. We don't get the gin and tonics anymore either, and the heating is on above in the house all the time now. Would them have anything to do with it?"

'"I think so. I'd say coming off the gin and tonic might be it," says he.

'"What?!" says I. "Malaria, is it? I have malaria?"

'"No," said the doctor, "you haven't malaria. You're an alcoholic."'

My mother was thrown by this revelation. 'But sure, I thought you didn't drink, Father?'

'I don't, and that's the reason why. It's the way it is for the rest of my life now. 'Tis one day at a time for me, man, and I'm better off for it,' he said, as he sucked life into another fresh Gold Flake from the glowing butt in his other hand. 'One fag at a time, sweet Jesus,' he laughed. 'If I can keep it down to that, I'll live till I die.'

And he was right. He did.

I loved Fr Casey and decided I wanted to be a priest like him when I grew up. But, to be honest,

I much preferred Santy to Jesus. On the way to fire stones at the rats in Carroll's Quay one day, I confided in my friend Henry Condon. I knew I could trust Henry. 'I was thinking that when I become a priest, I could start my own religion. It would be a religion for people like us, Henry, people who don't believe in God, but who do believe in Santy.'

Henry raised an eyebrow, so I gave him the full pitch.

'I mean, people wouldn't be expected to wait around thousands of years for the Second Coming, wondering if or when he's coming back. He'd be back every year. And we'd know exactly what date: the twenty-fourth of December every year, without fail.'

I could see from Henry's nodding that he was warming to the idea.

'There'd be no pictures in our churches of Santy being whipped or nailed to a cross. And there would only be three commandments: You'd better watch out. You'd better not pout. You'd better not cry.'

We both agreed I was on to something, but we also agreed that I had better keep the plan under wraps until after my ordination.

ooo

That Christmas, I became night-shift manager in the family shop, and I was ready for the challenge. If any drunks, robbers or brassers gave trouble in the shop after pub closing time, I'd wade into them with three mad dogs and a loaded hurley stick. That was the plan anyway. What's more, my older friend and next-door neighbour Seanie Carr would keep me company, perched on a pyramid of bags of coal outside the counter. Seanie was a cynic, always trying to convince me that there was no such thing as Santy.

On Christmas Eve, Seanie and I helped my father dress the crib in the shop window. Dad had built it in 1946 when my eldest sister, Norah, was a baby. By the time I had come along, many of the figures had been broken by tiny hands and replaced by substitutes from different Nativity sets. Indeed, our latest Saint Joseph was about eight times bigger than the donkey. But then, everything about my dad was big. He was a heavyweight, had the biggest family in the neighbourhood and owned an American car with three rows of seats. His heart was big too and often tested.

Our crib-dressing was interrupted by Christy's daily visit to the shop. Christy was a beggar by profession. He was good at it too. So every day at close of business, he would drop in to trade his copper stock for hard currency – notes and silver. But by the time he made it home to the Simon shelter via the off-licence, he would have liquidated his assets again.

Christy loved my dad and told him so regularly, especially when he was still locked. 'Mr Creedon, me old mate. You're the only one in the world who understands us. I love you, boy. I really do.'

However, he wasn't beyond biting the hand that fed him. As soon as we turned our backs to lift the crib into the window, Christy grabbed a huge armful of apples and oranges from the fruit display and tore off, my father shouting in his wake, 'The curse of Christ down on top of you anyway, Christy ... you, you, you ole bags, you!'

That night, as we locked up all the bolts and chains on the shop door, my father grumbled to himself, 'Jesus, they have my heart scalded. I haven't a thing left with 'em.'

A couple of hours later, I was lying in bed. Through the open doors I could hear my father in the next bedroom droning his way through the Rosary. As I teetered on that tightrope between watchfulness and sleep, a sudden rapping on the shop window downstairs jerked me awake.

Dad was first to spring into action. 'It's all right, I'll get it,' he whispered through the bedroom wall. *The hell you will*, I thought, as I grabbed my hurley stick and followed.

Having unlocked the bolt, the key lock and the safety chain, Dad opened the shop door to reveal his very best friend in the world.

'Mr Creedon, me oul' mate. How are they hangin'?' It was Christy, his arms laden with the stolen goods. 'You wouldn't have an oul' bag to put this lot into?' he said, nodding towards his armful of apples and oranges.

It had been several hours since we chased him off down Pine Street. He had probably shared a bottle of Cork Cream Sherry with his mates, fallen asleep and eventually come round wondering where the hell he had come by this fruit mountain. Then, in an attempt to summon some help from his 'best mate in de world', he unwittingly returned to the scene of the crime.

I looked at Christy, Dad looked at me, and Christy looked at both of us. Then my father spoke. 'John, a large bag for the gentleman, please, and don't delay.'

Confused, but relieved that Dad hadn't called my bluff and ordered me to wade into Christy with the hurley, I filled the bag.

'Steady up there now, go easy,' Dad told Christy. 'Keep in by the wall on the way home – and for God's sakes give up the oul' quare stuff for the New Year.'

'I will, Mr Creedon. You're me best mate, boy. All de best and have a great oul' Christmas now, the whole lot of ye.'

We returned to bed. Santy had yet to come, and as my father's snoring rattled the glass in the big old window frames, I got to thinking about the fun he knocked out of the whole drama with Christy. Then a shocking thought hit me: *What if my dad is the real Santy?*

I couldn't wait to tell Seanie Carr in the morning.

Aunty Theresa

Aunty Theresa was a tall, dark, delicate woman.

She said very little and seemed to observe the world nervously, sometimes with a worried look in her eyes. My mother's younger sister, she lived alone, and I once heard her tell Mrs Falvey in the chemist that she never married.

Theresa lived in the attic flat of a tall rickety house with bay windows. Each window was a grid of little square panes of thick glass, like something you might see on a Victorian Christmas card or a box of Quality Street. My mother said George Boole, the world-famous mathematician, once lived in that house and that Charles Dickens had visited him that time he gave a reading of *A Christmas Carol* in the Cork Opera House.

It would take me about twenty minutes to walk from our house along Camden Quay, Pope's Quay, North Mall and across the bridge at the foot of Sunday's Well to the house where Theresa lived. I dreaded the four-and-a-half flights of stairs to her door. The hallway and stairwell were pitch dark; there was no daylight and the landlord had taken out the fuse for the electric light. Theresa told me he only did it because he was heart-scalded from some tenant leaving the landing light on. Because I could see nothing in the dark, my pupils dilated and my ears attuned to every creak of the stairs and every groan of the house, alert to the slightest hint of movement in the shadows. I had to be ever ready for the day when the devil or Scrooge would jump out and grab me. Worse again, the Blessed Virgin could appear on the landing at any minute with a message for the world. She was doing that kind of thing to children all over the globe at the time.

My mother and father had helped Theresa find the flat. Before that, she had lived with us for a few years, and before that again she had spent a number of years in hospital.

My mother used to send my older sister Eugenia, with me by the hand, off on the bus with a bag of oranges to visit Aunty Theresa in the hospital. Sometimes she was in bed. Other times she'd be sitting in an armchair, wearing her beige cardigan, smoking and looking out the window. Sometimes she would talk to you, other times she wouldn't. But she was always nice to us. We didn't know why she was in hospital. I suppose it wasn't any of our business.

Apart from smoking, Theresa had no other hobbies, although she did write to *Ireland's Own* for the lyrics of a song on many occasions. She even had a letter published in their letters page once:

Dear Editor,

I enjoy your publication very much, especially Kitty the Hare, Cassidy and your jokes page, The Lilt of Irish Laughter.
I am requesting the words of 'Mellow the Moonlight/The Spinning Wheel' please. It was a very popular song in my childhood, but I seem to have forgotten some of the words. Perhaps you or your kind readers might be able to help me.
Yours sincerely,
Theresa Blake
(address with editor)

My mother carefully cut Theresa's contribution out of the letters page and put it into the photo album in her family letters drawer. She then stockpiled a dozen copies of said edition under the counter for safekeeping for 'future generations'. I was then immediately dispatched to Theresa's flat with a copy of said edition. Theresa didn't quite know what to make of her success. The reality of what she had gone and done landed heavily on her in the same way as it might a child who has spent a summer idly fishing by a stream, until one day, unexpectedly, they feel the terrible reality of a weighty tug on the other end of the line. A real fish is caught on the hook. There's no going back.

Theresa held the *Ireland's Own* at arm's length to see it better, and to keep some distance between herself and what she had done. I could hear her talking to herself from behind the opened magazine at the end of her outstretched arms: 'Wisha, God help us, I suppose I'm only making an oul' fool of myself,' she mumbled, as she quickly thumbed her way towards the letters page. When she arrived at the page, I could see her looking straight at me through the hole, her confused expression framed by the rectangular space as she attempted to process this latest disappointment. Unfortunately, I had brought the copy from which my mother had cut Theresa's letter for future generations, not an intact copy from the stockpile.

At least I hadn't just delivered it and left. God knows what she might have read into the one bit of the magazine that couldn't be read! She could have been stewing on some imagined reprimand from her sister about writing to the papers. I don't know, but it would certainly have preoccupied Theresa's mind until I got back from Scouts on Wednesday week. Who knew what would greet me on my next visit? However, Theresa was a very patient woman. I only hope that the 'future generations' my mother saved the magazine for will be equally generous, because I took a fresh copy from the stockpile intended for them and Theresa got an unblemished edition on my next courtesy call.

ooo

My father loved Theresa. He loved all of his nine sisters-in-law and they were all mad about him. 'Adrigole's favourite adopted son,' he'd say in a posh accent. 'That's what they used call me long 'go when I'd arrive back west to collect your mother. Adrigole's ... favourite ... adopted ... son ... ha?' he'd spell it out. 'How 'bout da'?' he'd say, savouring the accolade. 'Christ, your mother was a bombshell, but Theresa was a beautiful girl too. Tall and thin and very quiet. And her voice ... oh! If you could only get her to sing at all, she'd charm the birds out of the trees. She should have been out in Hollywood modelling.'

I remember him telling me, 'Theresa was a six-footer. She went to England, where she worked in a factory during the war. That's where she lost the top of her thumb in a loom.' My aunt wasn't quite 'a six-footer', but at about five foot eight, with her raven-black hair swept up in a bun, she wasn't too far off it.

And he was right about the modelling. I saw the photograph myself – in sepia tones like a piece of dust-bowl Americana, all these smiling young country girls fussing around my dad and his big swanky car, my mother wearing pleated trousers, leaning on the bonnet. All my aunts had big heads of hair and tiny waists. It was summertime so everyone had short sleeves. Theresa was there, tall and slender as a willow, smiling and squinting at the camera from under her salute to the sunshine.

Despite the harsh economics of growing up on a small farm of mountainy land in Beara, the 1940s was a romantic period and these girls clearly loved to giggle. Yes, there was rationing in Ireland and war in Europe, but this was also the heyday of Hollywood and dreams. There were adverts of women smoking and posters of men with broad shoulders with slicked-back hair selling Brylcreem.

When Theresa came to live with us, 30 years after that photograph was captured, she was still tall, but not as much. And she looked different. Her eyes now had a worried look that was exacerbated by mascara, crow's feet and the oily shine of Pond's Cold Cream.

The more my father loved you, the more he'd tease you. 'How's Split the Wind?' he'd say if he passed Theresa on the stairs at home. She'd laugh shyly and he'd follow up with, 'I hardly saw you there, Theresa. Christ, if you stood sideways you'd be marked absent. 'Tis out modelling you should be. You'd clean up! I'd do it myself, but they told me I'm too broad in the beam.' He'd laugh, delivering the final blow against himself.

Theresa didn't use the phone or drive a car, so any arrangement would have to be made in person. That's why I would never simply say, 'Goodbye' or 'All the best, Theresa, talk soon,' just in case she thought she'd never see you again. I would have to be clear and say something like 'I'm going down to Johnny Creedon's to help him with the hay, but I'll call up to you on Saturday week after tea.'

'Oh, that would be lovely, *peteen bán*, and maybe we could go to the pictures if it's not a school night?'

'No, Theresa, we never go to school on Sundays.'

'That's right,' she'd say.

On Saturday week, I'd arrive and she'd be sitting there, looking out the window at a flotilla of swans gliding effortlessly through the choppy winter wavelets on the North Channel of the Lee. Above the surface, the swans, like Theresa, were calm and graceful. She would be ready and waiting in her mauve overcoat, which was secured with a broad black patent belt, wearing matching shoes and bag. Sometimes she'd wear a turquoise turban and other times she'd just wear her ordinary woollen hat with the bobble.

We'd sit there and she'd ask, 'Are you being a good boyeen?'

'I am.'

'How are you getting on in school?'

'Grand.'

'Is your teacher cross?'

'Yes, he's still cross. The same as when you asked me last week.'

'And how's Mammy?'

'Grand.'

'And how's Daddy?'

'Grand. And how are you, Theresa?'

'Grand.'

When she was in form for it, Theresa would bring me to the pictures. She'd always buy us a bag of Iced Caramels and a bag of Scots Clan and we'd discuss the film on the way home.

There were a lot of holy films doing the rounds back then. They were very good, like, but I'd always close my eyes when God showed up or if he got tortured. Anyway, they say you should never look directly into the eyes of God.

Quo Vadis was about Emperor Nero, who was bad with the nerves and really cruel to the Christians. Theresa told me the Christians lived thousands of years ago and got killed off by the Romans. I told her I wasn't gone on the Christians myself. I didn't like the way they were always hiding behind each other and getting pushed around by the Romans. I much preferred the Romans. They were brilliant at marching and fighting and they wore red miniskirts and helmets with a red brush on top. Theresa told me the red bushy thing was to make them look taller and to scare the Christians.

The Romans caught St Peter and crucified him upside down in front of a huge crowd just to teach him a lesson. Our teacher used to slap us in front of the class to teach us a lesson, but I didn't think you would learn much of a lesson if you were crucified upside down. The crowd only jeered poor St Peter.

There was also a huge crowd in the Coliseum the day Ben-Hur won the chariot race. Charlton Heston was Ben-Hur and the Coliseum was a cinema on MacCurtain Street.

Everyone in Cork called the Coliseum 'The Col', and while there was often a crush to get in, the crush for *Ben-Hur* was deadly. Aunty Theresa said we should wait and when the crush was gone in, we'd follow it. *Ben-Hur* went on for ages, but the chariot race and the gladiators fencing and fighting each other were brilliant. And at least during the boring talking bits I was able to chomp away on the Iced Caramels, happy out for myself. The film was so long that there was an intermission, so we went out to the toilet, but we didn't get anymore sweets for after the break. I think Theresa had no money left and all I had in my pocket was a penny for school on Monday morning, and I couldn't spend that because it was for the black babies. Afterwards, in our 'discussion' about the film, we both agreed that it was very good, but way too long.

The Palace Cinema was also on MacCurtain Street and it was amazing. It was only two shop-fronts wide at street level, but once you went in the front doors the hallway led you in and in and in ... all the way to the double doors that opened into a red-velvet paradise. The balcony rose steeply to the rafters, and the proscenium arch that surrounded the screen was embossed in gold scrolling. Four private boxes with domes, each topped by a spear-like point, towered above the stage. They looked to me like a Turkish minaret or a policeman's helmet.

We went to the Palace to see *The Song of Bernadette*. That was fierce sad altogether. A teenager called Bernadette, who lived in Lourdes, had a really cross teacher who mocked her. But the Blessed Virgin appeared to her out of the blue and told her not to be scared and gave her a message for the world. She said, 'I am the Immaculate Conception.' But Bernadette's parents and the whole town didn't believe her, which is the worst thing you can do to a child. When someone doesn't believe you, especially when you are really telling the truth, it would make you want to run away to another country.

By the time the house lights came up, we were both traumatised by the terrible sadness and holiness of it all. I, with my trembling lower lip, was petrified at the possibility of the Blessed Virgin looking down from the screen and picking someone from the audience to whom she would appear later in the week. I caught Theresa dabbing a tear with her glove as the lights came up. I could see from her mascara that she must have been crying earlier in the film too.

My dad said Theresa wasn't the first person to come out of the Coliseum with a black eye.

We went to see *Goldfinger* when it came in, too. The old lady in the sweet shop told us, 'The new James Bond filum is very popular.'

'And what is James Bond all about?' Theresa enquired. 'If it's about cowboys or Romans this maneen might enjoy it.'

'I don't know,' the sweet-shop lady replied, 'but there is an actress with an Irish name in it.'

'Who? Grace Kelly?'

'No,' she replied, wracking her brain for the answer.

'Maureen O'Hara?'

'No,' she continued.

'Who?'

'I never heard of her before,' the sweet-shop lady replied. 'Her name is Pussy Galore.'

No, Aunty Theresa and I had never heard of her before either, but we decided to give her the benefit of the doubt. Theresa bought a package of Rothmans from the sweet-shop lady and asked me if I'd like Iced Caramels. I said that if she didn't mind, I'd like a package of the chocolate sweetie cigarettes instead.

It was cold in the Palace that night, but we were happy out, puffing away on our cigarettes and taking turns to tap the ash from our fags into the little silver ashtray that was screwed onto the back of the seats in front of us. Because my cigarette was chocolate, I made sure not to actually touch the top of it against the ash in the ashtray. Just pretend.

James Bond came on and he was English, not Roman. He wasn't a cowboy either, but he had a gun and a ring for poisoning the baddies. But then a girl came on and she had only her swimming togs on. Not togs like the girls up the baths in Cork. No, this was a bikini and you could see nearly everything.

I decided I didn't want to see anything, especially as my aunty was sitting beside me and she was fierce holy altogether. So, I did what I did when Jesus was being tortured – I looked away. By the time James Bond went into the bedroom with Pussy Galore, we were both looking anywhere else and chain-smoking our fags.

All around us the heat was rising from a hundred glowing cigarettes and another hundred glowing courting couples. As the temperature in the cinema rose, so too did the bobble hat on Theresa's head. Maybe it was the combination of the heat, her shiny black hair and the wool, but her hat began to ride up on her head to the point where the pom-pom at the top was several feet above her shoulders. Eventually it was a full six foot four inches above sea level.

Two teenagers behind us started kicking the back of Theresa's seat. In the flickering light from the screen, I could see that she didn't know which way to look, but she did know *how* to look. Frightened.

I knew I hadn't a hope, but I lost the plot completely. I stubbed out my nearly full chocolate cigarette, turned around quickly and shouted, 'Cop on! Leave her seat alone. She's my aunty and she never did nothin' to no one.'

'Yeah? Well tell yer aunty I can't see Pussy Galore with her fuckin' hat.'

Theresa put out her fag, got up and moved over to the aisle seat closest to the exit. I followed, our two flip-up seats banging to a chorus of shushes and one roar of 'Will ye shut up?!'

We were both bewildered and totally disconnected from the film. Me because of what the boys were saying behind us and Theresa because of what Pussy Galore was saying in front of us. No sooner had we sat down in our new seats than she was up and off again. This time straight out the double doors under the exit sign. I followed her.

At the corner of Bridge Street and home, she let go of my hand and spoke for the first time since the usherette had shown us to our seats. 'Will you be OK from here, peteen?'

'I will. Will you be OK?'

'I will.'

'OK so, I'll call over to you on Wednesday on my way to Scouts. Do you want me to bring anything with me from home?'

'No. Bye-bye now. Good boy.'

'Bye-bye, Theresa. Thanks a million.'

We never discussed that film. Ever. In fact, we never went to the pictures together again.

Eurovision

It was 1967. I was eight and had just recently quit the fags. I had been a casual smoker from about the age of five or six. Mrs McCarthy up in the Iveleary Bar would let me light one of her Carrolls for her, and Aunty Abbie up on Patrick's Hill, who wasn't my aunt at all, was always good for a drag off her Woodbine. Mrs Shortt wouldn't let me: 'Get away, ye cheeky pup. Coffin nails, that's all these are. If I hear you asking for a puff off a fag again, 'tis your mother and father I'll be telling.'

Mrs Shortt, who survived on a diet of tea, fags and bags of cut-price broken biscuits, also told me I wouldn't grow and that I'd be small forever. In fairness, she was walking proof of her own theory. 'Shortt be name and short be stature,' she'd say. 'I'm donatin' me body to science when I die. Up to UCC I'll be goin' – 'tis the only way the likes of me will ever get into college. And if you're not careful, you'll be in the same class as me.' That did it. I quit within a few days.

But when I was smoking, I'd smoke anything. I once smoked a soft-drink straw that I had hobbled out of our shop when my mam wasn't watching. I brought it upstairs to the sitting room, switched on the two-bar electric heater, and when I was sure I was alone, I pushed one end of the waxed white straw through the guard grille and touched the glowing top bar. Yes, it worked! The top of my cigarette caught fire. I placed the other end to my pursed lips and with my brow furrowed against a stray wisp of smoke to the eye, I inhaled deeply. I felt like the Marlboro Man when round-up was done on the prairie. Yes siree, I sucked in a good lungful of flame, ash and molten wax. I don't remember much more of that incident, but when I came around, my sister Eugenia gave me a packet of chocolate buttons to cheer me up.

On another occasion, for a dare, I pushed a kitchen knife through the safety grille to touch the same glowing orange bar. All I remember of that one was the bang and a thud of dull pain punching me in the arm. I heard my mother and father talking again about 'farming him out, for his own safety'.

Anyway, there I was, off the fags and doing my best to be good. It can't have been a school night because I was helping my mother in the shop when he came in. I didn't see him at first, as I was over on the far side of the shop, arranging the rows of tins of Russian salad and potato salad before I moved on to straightening the jars of carrots and beetroot and Branston pickle on the shelf above them. I was preparing the guard of honour for my mother's inspection later. Shoulder to shoulder they stood, in neat rows, all labels facing outwards. Eyes front!

The door bell chinged, but my mother was at the till, so I paid it little heed. Then I heard the voice ... and that rang a bell. A somehow familiar soft Dublin accent deep-soaked in a luxurious baritone greeted my mother. 'Hello there.' Even the greeting sounded familiar.

As I turned to see if it could really be him, I realised my mother had the exact same hunch, and she replied, 'Hello ... Seán, is it?'

I was right. She was right. It was actually Seán Dunphy and the Hoedowners, but without the Hoedowners. He had left the band sound-checking across the road in the Hilton while he nipped across to the shop, our shop, for a packet of smokes. The Hoedowners were fab – they had their own TV show on RTÉ every week.

Seán Dunphy was tall and tanned and mannerly. I was weak in the presence of beauty and too shy to say anything during our encounter. Apart, that is, from one letter and one number.

My mother nodded in my general direction and said, 'John's your biggest fan in Cork.'

'Is that a fact? Good man. What class are you in?'

'3B,' I whispered.

'Good man yourself,' he smiled.

My mother told Seán that I collected pop pictures and had Roly Daniels's and Brendan Bowyer's autographed photos.

'I'd say the boys will have a few pics in the van,' he said, smiling at me. 'I'll try to drop back with one later.'

He never did.

We mopped the shop floor, bolted the door and switched off the lights a little later than usual that night. As I said goodnight and turned for the stairs, my mother asked if I was all right and said, 'He might not have had a chance with the huge crowds over.'

'I know. It was deadly meeting him, though. Goodnight, Mam.'

In bed, I processed the encounter. I'd be able to tell the boys in 3B on Monday that I met Seán Dunphy and that I told him all about our class. *I wish I had the pop pic, though, 'cause Sullivan will say I'm making it all up. He'll say, 'Where's the proof?' like he always does.*

Weekends were always good in our place. My father would pull in the huge bundles of newspapers and magazines left at the door by the News Brothers delivery van, and Friday's comics could be read before they reached their intended paying customers. *Dandy* and *Bunty* arrived on Monday, *Beano* and *Judy* on Wednesday, but on Friday it was older boys' comics like *Hornet*, *Victor* and *Valiant*. I loved those ones, where the Germans would capture an '*Englisher* pig-dog' and be just about to bayonet the defenceless Tommy in the belly when another Nazi would roar, '*Achtung! Achtung! Englishers!*' as a load of good guys would jump into the foxhole and bate the head off the Nazis, shouting, 'Take that, Jerry!' Then the Jerrys would put their hands up, crying, '*Kamerad. Kamerad.*'

This particular morning, I was turning the page to see if the captain would execute the Jerrys or send them back to Blighty to be POWs, when a leaflet advertising a free offer fell out. Except it wasn't a free offer – it was a large black-and-white photograph of Seán Dunphy and the Hoedowners, with a swish of blue marker across the bottom that read, 'To my very good friend John, from Seán Dunphy.' The swirl of the 'S' in the 'Seán' was magnificent, and he had put in the *síneadh fada* and all. The smell of chemicals from the marker was beautiful.

I looked up and my father was standing over me, smiling. He winked and said, 'He must have pushed it in under the shop door at some God-unearthly hour of the morning. I was wondering how long it would take you to find it in the comics. I knew full well you'd never find it if I stuck it into your schoolbooks!'

'Deadly! Does Mam know?'

'Not yet, but you can tell her yourself when she gets up. She told me going to bed last night that he was in and that ye were both disappointed he didn't call back. I was rightly impressed to find he slipped it under the shop door.'

When my mother heard the news, she was delighted that Seán had honoured his word, and

Margaret, who worked in our shop and shared my passion for pop pics, said it was probably a collector's item because it had both names on it: mine and Seán's. We decided there and then that we were all going to cheer for him in the National Song Contest, which would be on the telly on 12 February.

The kitchen was packed that night. Brendan O'Reilly was the presenter. He was really famous. He won the long jump and read sports news and could sing too, but not as good as the contestants – they were the best in the whole country. We all loved Johnny McEvoy and Patricia Cahill, who had both been in the competition before.

'She did very well there a few years ago,' said Miss Healy, our shop assistant. 'Johnny Creedon was in earlier to collect the waste and he said Patricia Cahill was in it a few years ago with a song called "I Stand Still".'

'I don't remember that one at all,' Aunty Theresa chipped in, 'but I'd say 'twas good too.'

''Twas,' said Miss Healy, 'and Johnny Creedon said the song Seán Dunphy is singing tonight was written by the same lad who writes *Tolka Row*.'

'Is that a fact?' asked Theresa.

'Yes. It's in the *RTV Guide*. "If I Could Choose" written by Wesley Burrowes and Michael Coffey and sung by Seán Dunphy.' I loved the way Miss Healy still called it the *RTV Guide*, even though it had changed its name to the *RTÉ Guide* the year before and we stocked it in the shop.

'Deirdre O'Callaghan has a lovely song in this year too. I heard Mike Murphy playing it on *Music on the Move*.'

'Whisht, let ye!' said Dad. 'Seán Dunphy is coming on next.'

On he came, and he was brilliant.

When he got to the chorus, we knew he was in with a great chance.

> *If I could choose [de ne ne neh, de ne ne neh]*
> *a time to talk with you [de ne ne neh, de ne ne neh]*
> *I'd choose the longest day*
> *And over all the hills of Clare, I'd shout the news*
> *I would tell them how a day could last forever*
> *And I'd never leave your side, if I could choose.*

When all the contestants had performed, Brendan O'Reilly reminded the folks watching at home that 'the final decision rests with you. The winner will be decided by postal vote, so send your vote, along with your name and address on a postcard or sealed envelope, to National Song Contest, RTÉ, Montrose, Donnybrook, Dublin Four.'

I suggested we send in a load of them with pretend names and addresses, but my mother insisted that we do it the honest way and send in just one postcard for each person in the house. So Eugenia and myself were sent up to MacCurtain Street post office to buy the 18 stamps and then walk on the extra few yards to post all the cards in Brian Boru Street sorting office. We needed to make sure they'd reach Brendan O'Reilly in good time.

My older siblings all loved *Pop Call*, hosted by Val Joyce. In the years before television was widespread, *Pop Call* was huge. The format was simple: a pop-music request show that followed a strict A-to-Z sequence. So every time it was coming around to the letter C again, poor old Val was bombarded with postcards from the C-for-Creedons. It worked a few times and we were the talk of the town the next morning.

'I heard ye on *Pop Call* last night. Val managed to pronounce all the names right again this time, even Eugenia.'

Seán's song was played on *Pop Call*.

The following week, the results were announced. Seán had walked away with it.

On Monday in school, Brother Gill asked me to stand up. 'Seán Ó Críodáin, *seas suas*. Your friend did us proud on Saturday evening. Well done. I hope he goes all the way for us now and does well in Europe.' I felt I was on 'Team Seán' and I had a bounce in my step, hoping people would stop me and ask me about Seán and what he was really like.

It was all the talk in the shop too. 'He's doing rehearsals above in Dublin,' said Hannie Mac.

'Noel Kelehan will be travelling to conduct the orchestra for Seán's song and he's an excellent conductor. So at least that will be a big help to him,' added Mrs Shortt.

Johnny Creedon was at the counter having one of his long chats with Miss Healy, and he put the whole challenge in a nutshell: 'Oh, this will be the tough one now. The National Song Contest is like the All-Ireland, but the Eurovision? That will be like the World Cup.'

We all agreed.

ooo

A few days later, I was at the kitchen table, struggling with my sums, when I heard my dad calling me from the shop. 'Come out, your namesake is here and he's got something to show you.'

Johnny Creedon was outside the counter and had a parcel wrapped in brown paper under his arm.

'Here,' he said, handing me the package. 'Take the string off that and have a look and tell us what you think,' he said proudly. I took the parcel and it felt like there was something hard, about the same size as our kettle, inside the wrapper. I eventually untied the knot and unwrapped the paper.

'Jesus, don't drop it!' they both warned, as a cream-coloured slender vase with two small loop handles at the neck emerged from the wrapping.

'Christ, that's a Grecian urn!' declared my father. 'That's probably priceless!'

'I don't know about that,' shrugged Johnny, equally impressed, 'but I can assure you of one thing. It is most definitely the Glounthaune Donkey Derby Perpetual Trophy.'

I couldn't believe my eyes. This was it. I was actually holding it. I had the prize in my hands. Not for long, though.

'Give it back here to me. Carefully now. I need to get it back to the committee before eight o'clock tonight, or they'll have a search party out looking for me.'

I carefully handed over the object of all my desires and Johnny said his goodbyes. 'I'll collect you on Friday night and you can train away all weekend if you like.'

'Brilliant. I'll be ready.'

I so wanted to win that trophy and put it on a shelf in the shop.

I turned to my father. 'Can you imagine, Dad, if I won the donkey derby and Seán won the Eurovision? That would be amazing, wouldn't it?'

My father smiled. 'Stranger things have happened.'

I wondered if Seán was as nervous about his big day as I was about mine.

ooo

My sister Norah told us on the phone that a busload of supporters was going out on a plane from Dublin Airport to cheer for Seán. 'Mostly family and neighbours from around Whitehall,' she said.

'And surely RTÉ will send another couple out along with Noel Kelehan,' added my brother Don. Our kitchen was buzzing.

'He'll have good travelling support so.'

'He'll need it all. He won't be getting it easy out there.'

'That's for sure. Austria is no joke.'

As usual, the bookies were tipping Britain. Sandie Shaw was all the rage and people who had heard her song, 'Puppet on a String', said it was really catchy. Typical. I wouldn't have minded so much, but her song was co-written by a man from Northern Ireland called Phil Coulter. I mean, that's not fair. What hope would we have when we'd put in two songs, but only one of them could win it for us? Why were we helping the UK when they never did anything except torment us?

Louie Angelini dropped in from the bookie's next door to collect his daily supply of English newspapers and *The Sporting Life*. The racing pages would be pinned to the wall of the bookie's for old fellas to squint at and study the form.

Dad asked Louie if he had any idea how the Eurovision might go.

'Och, ah dinnae ken, Con. Sandie Shaw will be hard tae beat, but tha' wee Greek lassie singin' furr Luxembourg is a right daurk horse with an ootside chonce a' takin' it.'

My father translated for us. 'Louie is saying that, apart from Sandie Shaw, Vicky Leandros from Athens has a slim chance of winning it for Luxembourg.'

'L'amour Est Bleu' was Vicky's song and I had heard it several times. My sisters were singing it around the house in both French and English, day and night. Some help to Ireland they were!

It wasn't looking good at all for Seán, but my dad still had a hunch about him. 'If Ireland ever gets to win the Eurovision, this is it. This is the one chance we have.'

There were 17 countries in the contest and we were one of the smallest. Ireland was drawn to sing last, but Seán was handsome and steady as a rock, so we still had a chance.

The big night was to be in Vienna, and thanks to satellite television, the big night was also to be in our kitchen. Mrs Shortt said she heard that it would be shown to an audience of thousands all over Europe. Someone else said this was the last year it would only be transmitted in black and white, that next year some countries would be able to put it out in colour. It was on the news that Portugal's contestant was going to be the first black man to ever sing in the competition – a fella called Eduardo Nascimento. We all agreed that it would be a great night's work if Eduardo did well too and came in second or even third after Seán.

Like all big nights, it took its time arriving, and when it finally came, it didn't feel like a big night at first. The shop was closed. Miss Healy and Margaret both had the night off. But as curtain-up approached, the entire household got restless as we gathered in the kitchen.

'Bring down another two chairs.'

'Is your Fanta all gone?'

"Tis. Can I have another one?'

'Yerra go on, and bring in a few bags of crisps too.'

My mother was worried for Seán. She said that he might be nervous going last. Theresa added to the pressure when she said that the food in Europe mightn't suit him.

The Eurovision test card came on the screen, wobbled a bit, but then it was grand again as the prelude to Charpentier's 'Te Deum' blasted through the speaker on the side of our Pye television.

'Blast-off!' said Dad. 'Where's your mother?' He threw his voice up the stairs. 'Siobhán, 'tis on now!'

My mother said she was changing the sheets, but really she was too nervous to watch it. Instead, she was listening to it on the wireless in their bedroom.

Margaret, Miss Healy, Aunty Theresa, five or six siblings and myself were packed into the kitchen. Like a colony of gannets, our family had developed a system whereby everyone could talk and be heard at the same time. We could all tune to whatever frequency was required to continue a private chat amidst the dissonance. Furthermore, we were always free to speak our minds, so everyone would commentate freely on whatever was on television, even when the event already came complete with a commentator.

Everyone in the room had an opinion when the showjumping was on, and Michael O'Hehir rarely got a word in beyond the greetings to listeners in Boston and New York at the start of an All-Ireland Final before he was eclipsed by the Creedons of Cork, who would take it away once 'Amhrán na bhFiann' reached its crescendo. Michael O'Hehir was duty-bound to stay silent at that point. Tonight we were all ready for whatever Austria could throw at us.

'*Mesdames et messieurs*,' began Erica Vaal, the presenter.

'Get on with it!' we shouted.

The action continued in Vienna despite intermittent interruptions from Cork.

'That girl has a fine voice.'

'That oul' dress doesn't do much for her.'

'Shhh!'

'When is Seán coming on?'

'Will you shut up?!'

'You shut up.'

'Will ye both shut up and hiren the telly?!'

Then Erica said it. '*Et maintenant l'Irlande* ...'

'Christ, we're on!'

'Shaw-in Doonfee ...'

'Who?'

'... *avec "Si Je Pouvais Choisir"*/"If I Could Choose".'

'G'wan Seánnieee boyyyy!'

Theresa looked anxious at this stage.

The conductor raised his baton. We took our cue and the kitchen fell silent.

There he was, all six foot of him – the hopes of a nation in a tuxedo with stylish satin lapels and a dickie bow, hands demurely by his sides, standing behind a solitary mic stand.

A drum roll.

The Austrian State Orchestra opened the song with a brass fanfare and then an intro of sweeping strings to bring the melody, on a cushion, to our Seán.

A pause.

We all held our breath as Seán released his.

> *They envy me, my hills of Clare*
> *The white gulls calling in the soft sea air*
> *So much to lose*
> *And yet I'd leave the hills of Clare*
> *and live in a desert if I had you there*
> *What would I lose if I could choose?*
> [*de neh neh neh … de neh neh neh*]

He was majestic, cool and controlled. Then came the key change, and as he sang, 'Bellows by the fire, and the turf smoke rising higher', Seán raised his eyes to the studio lights above him as if he were thinking of us all sitting around the fire back in Ireland. As he rounded the bend for the home straight, he looked right down the lens of the camera and winked, like he was winking at some lucky shop assistant in a crowded ballroom back home.

And then the big finish. With Noel Kelehan driving the orchestra on to even greater heights, they lifted Seán on golden wings as he soared above the Austrian Alps with outstretched arms. 'If I could … choooooose!'

Then, to thunderous applause, he dropped from the waist into a bow, as if he had collapsed from exhaustion.

Each country had a total of ten points to distribute amongst the other entries as it saw fit. The voting was a disaster. There were loads of mistakes with the scoreboard and Erica Vaal had to correct it a few times. We all felt sorry for her, especially when the English jury spokesman made a smart remark about it.

I looked enviously at Aunty Theresa, who was temptingly lighting one fag off the last.

When the UK phoned in their vote, what did they give to poor old Seán? '*Deux points.*' Two measly points.

Gay Byrne came on the phone to give the Irish vote. A big cheer went up in the kitchen.

'G'wan, Gay!' said Marie-Thérèse.

'Give Seán all ten of 'em!' I added.

'You can't vote for yourself,' my dad explained to me.

'Why not? Seán is the best thing in it.'

'Because you can't, that's all. Whisht!'

In the finish, Sandie Shaw ran away with it. She was well over the finishing line, and the Germans, who had been at war with Britain just over 20 years earlier, were actually voting for them. God almighty! Sandie Shaw and your man from Northern Ireland got first place with 47 points, with Vicky Leandros coming in fourth for Luxembourg. But Seán Dunphy came second!

We were all roaring as loud as we could. I ran out onto the street cheering at the exact same time as the McAuliffes came pouring out of No. 16. The Corcorans were out moments later.

'There's only three million people in the whole Republic of Ireland and we hammered France and Germany and Spain,' shouted Theo McAuliffe.

Later, from my bedroom, I could hear the corner boys going home from the pub, and they were all singing, 'If I could choose, de ne ne neh, de ne ne neh.'

I couldn't sleep. My good friend Seán had just nearly won the Eurovision. How about that? Ireland that had never *nearly* won anything, and here we were *nearly* winning the Eurovision.

If Ireland ever wins anything, I hope we all remember Seán Dunphy. I made a pledge to myself before I finally drifted off. *I will always remember 8 April 1967, the night Seán Dunphy came second and I nearly went back on the fags.*

One to Stop

'One to stop. Two to go.' Ordinary people knew the first bit. That was easy. It was written beside the roundy red bell above the handrail. But my dad, his conductor and my good self all knew the full code. When I wasn't farmed out to Johnny, my dad would often take me to work with him.

Like my mam, my dad worked hard. Too hard. As soon as he came in from his shift, he would release my mother from shop duties and take over. At weekends, he'd clock up some overtime on the Bingo Bus to Bandon, or on a 'Drop Special', which in essence was a day trip to the seaside at Crosshaven or Kinsale. But my dad was mostly driving city routes for CIÉ in a standard-issue cream-and-navy Leyland Titan double-decker bus. He sat in a separate half-cab up the front, beside the piping-hot engine. The half-cab was accessed by its own little door at the front. He was completely cut off from the saloon and the only means of communication, apart from the bell which would ding beside him in the cab, was the small sliding glass window at his back. A bench seat ran the width of the bus, back-to-back with the driver. On a quiet run, his conductor could kneel on the bench, slide back the glass and chat away to the back of my father's head, like in Confession. There were also two bench seats running lengthways just inside the rear of the saloon. These were usually occupied by men, while ladies preferred to sit in the regular forward-facing seats, and teenagers grabbed the back seats upstairs. The conductor had a series of mirrors around the bus that he used to keep an eye out for fare-dodgers and troublemakers.

Each route took the bus on a two-hour, figure-eight circuit across the city from Northside to Southside and back through Patrick Street, the narrowest point in the figure eight. From there it would depart on its second loop to the opposite side of the city, then back again to Patrick Street to repeat the circuit. There were about twenty such routes and they almost all went up along the Northside and out along the Southside. The No. 3 went out around Ballyphehane and back through Pana up to Farranree. The No. 8 went all the way to Bishopstown before it returned to dissect the figure eight and head up the steep climb to Mayfield. From the top of the ridge that runs all along the Northside, you could look down on the underbelly of the city – the Southside – with its ever-expanding suburbs of Douglas, Grange, Togher, Wilton and Bishopstown. They had shopping centres out there. The Northside had none. We usually had a cluster of shops around a post office here and there, like in Sunday's Well, Blackpool, Shandon Street and Saint Luke's. Small purpose-built shopping malls arrived with the newer estates. Big suburban shopping centres only began to appear in the 1970s. The next ring of new estates to circle the city, such as Mahon and Knocknaheeny and Hollyhill, had yet to be born – just like the people who now call them home.

My favourite route, though, was the No. 14: the rollercoaster route. Upstairs front row was the best seat in the house for this adventure. I would sometimes pretend it was the donkey derby and that I was steering Rosie, leaning hard left around the bend as we raced for the final furlong and the finish line.

The bus would gather momentum along the North Mall for the blind bend that introduces the steep sweep up Sunday's Well Road. There was no point in a half-hearted attempt at the wall of death, as the bus might stall and you really didn't want to be reversing a double-decker back downhill against the traffic coming up. We spent half our time push-starting stalled cars, but a bus?

The real test came on the homeward journey. The double S-bend at the bottom of Douglas Street on the final approach to Summerhill South was a feat of strength for any driver in the pre-power-steering age. But my dad was a big man and the best driver in Ireland at the time. He would approach the acute chicane at full throttle to swing the double-decker around the two corners. It was hard-a-starboard then immediately hard-a-port ... and before you could shout 'Christ!' it was hard-a-starboard again and he'd rev up the hill as you tried to pick yourself up from the floor.

His regular conductor, Mick Cronin, would let me wear his hat, turn the handle on the ticket machine and shout, 'Fares please!' When we reached the terminus, he would allow me to open the little wooden door to wind the handle on the roller on the inside that changed the destination display on the outside. He also gave me the full bell code: one to stop and two to go. There was a bell midway down the lower deck, another upstairs and one hidden bell under the stairs in the conductor's caboose, which Mick pronounced 'caw-boosh'. Ordinary people were only allowed to press the other two bells and to press only once if they wished to alight at the next stop. 'Two to go' was the preserve of the conductor only, or me with his approval.

My father's colleagues Mick McGrath and Paul 'Popeye' O'Neill always turned a blind eye to the sight of an unaccompanied minor wandering around the bus station or peeping out the window of a locked bus. I knew how to open the door from the outside and how to close it from the inside, just in case anyone tried to rob it. I expect my father wouldn't have troubled CIÉ for compensation anyway if I had tumbled down the stairs or fallen off the open platform onto the road. His first priority, I would hope, would be to notice I was actually missing. A glance in the bus's two big ears – the wing mirrors – would confirm that, yes, the sudden peace and quiet on the bus was because I had been launched off the back.

No one ever fell off his bus, but a man in a suit fell *onto* the bus once. My enthusiasm for the job got the better of me. I jumped the gun and pressed 'two to go' before the conductor's say-so. The coast was clear, or so I thought, but this late arrival was running and just reaching for the rail to steady himself as he hopped aboard. However, on my double-ding, Dad released the clutch, the bus lurched forward and yer man hit the deck on his hands and knees. At first he was rightly hot and bothered about his 'dignity', but Mick eventually convinced him that it was all his own fault 'for attempting to board a moving vehicle, without due care or consideration'. He neglected to mention that the real culprit was an eight-year-old in a bus conductor's hat hiding in the 'caw-boosh' under the stairs.

As soon as yer man got off, my father pulled in, climbed out of the cab and came around the back to us for the steward's enquiry. 'God blasht you! You'll cost me my job. Is it up in Shandon steeple bell-ringing you think you are? That's enough of the bell-ringing for one day. Jesus forgive me my sins, you could have killed the man. What would we tell your mother then?'

I spent 20 minutes alone in the ladies' seats downstairs, silenced by the lump in my throat. The reality of what I had done was beginning to sink in – I had nearly murdered a man. My parents had warned me more than once that I was far too arch for my own good and that I'd end up in a reformatory. As we passed Blackrock Church, I asked God to stop me being so arch, just as I did most nights in bed. 'Please, God, stop me being so arch and help me to calm down before I do things that get me in trouble' or 'Please, Jesus, I know you like kids, can you just give me a warning sign before I do something stupid. Just whisper "One to stop" or something like that?'

But forgiveness came easy to my dad, and I was known for a quick recovery, so on the way back to the garage, Mick and myself were kneeling at the bus's confessional window and giving the action replay to the back of my father's head.

'Yerra, a pity about him and his dignity,' said Mick.

'Pride comes before a fall,' says I.

As we pulled into the yard in Capwell, Mick posed his fellow crew members a riddle. 'What goes "Ding, ding, ouch"?'

'What?' roared my dad over the sound of the engine. 'What goes ding, ding, ouch, is it? I've no idea. What is it?'

'A crew of Creedons on a bus!' roared Mick.

'I was thinking,' says I, 'do ye know why I don't want to be a conductor when I grow up?'

They both paused at my announcement.

'Why?' asked Mick.

'Well, I was thinking that the money's all right, but it's the same ding-dong every day.'

Then we all roared laughing.

My dad gave me a second glance, a kind of proud look, as if he was thinking, 'The small fella is as funny as myself!'

The Orange Curtain

In 1968, I was nine and my parents announced that we were going on a family holiday. Apart from being farmed out to Johnny Creedon and cousins in the country, I had never been on holidays. I mean real holidays, with your mam and dad and ice cream and stuff.

When my older siblings were small and my parents were young, they would rent a bungalow in Myrtleville or book a place in Trabolgan for a week or two by the sea. But us younger ones had never experienced a family holiday, as such.

On this occasion, my dad arrived home with a 10-berth caravan. At least he convinced my mother it was a 10-berth caravan. Either way, it was huge: three sets of bunk beds, a jacks, a gas cooker, orange and yellow cushions, and orange curtains patterned with huge sunflowers. Dad had a fine big old red-and-cream Mercedes, complete with a ball hitch, so we were game ball to go.

The anticlockwise circuit of Ireland my dad planned for the trip would afford us an opportunity to meet up with all four siblings who were working away from home. First, we would meet with Norah and Carol Ann. Norah was working with Munster & Leinster Bank and Carol Ann had started nursing training at St Vincent's Hospital, so they were both in Dublin. Then we would go on to Meath, where Vourneen was working as a lifeguard at Butlin's, Mosney. Mam had targeted Belfast for the Twelfth of July parades, and that would be followed by a trip down the west coast. Constance was working at a hotel in Kenmare in County Kerry for the summer and that would be our penultimate stop on our way back to Cork.

The fact that none of us had any caravanning experience was immaterial, because my mam and dad were brilliant at everything. Also, because there were so many of us, four of the children would travel in the back seat of the car and the rest would travel in the caravan.

However, the road to Belfast was paved with tears. Our parents drove us around the country and we drove them around the bend. Every time we opened the caravan window when cooking to let the smoke out, the gas went out. Every time we closed the window, the smoke filled the caravan, and we all ran out – then the gas ran out.

On day one, we met the two girls in Dublin and went to the zoo, where a baby chimp pooped on Norah at the chimps' tea party. We parked up at Malahide beach, where most of us got sunburned. After a night of our whingeing, my parents packed up for the road to Mosney. If we had any sense, we'd have all packed up and gone home, but, undeterred, we took off again. However, a mile or so up the road, the horrific truth landed with a crash in the caravan. We hadn't packed up at all. Well, not properly, anyway. As we gathered speed and rounded the first proper bend on the Belfast road, drawers, coat hangers, cutlery and children went flying.

My father's age-old mantra of 'put that away before you knock someone's eye out' had come back to haunt him. As my sisters ducked the flying knives, I was dispatched to try to alert my parents. I was flung mercilessly from side to side by the rocking and rolling caravan. Dad used to also say, 'Come down off that or you'll break your neck.' Now here he was, running the risk of breaking our necks and knocking our eyes out.

I climbed up on the front window seat, desperately holding on to the swaying orange curtains as my father rounded the bend at Balbriggan. Pounding the caravan's front window with my little fists, I screamed, 'Maaam! Daaad! Stop the car! Pleeease stop the car!'

No reaction. Nothing, except the back of my siblings' heads swaying from side to side to their own little sing-song in the back seat of the car. There was nothing for it but to retreat to the bedroom and hide in a wardrobe until the nightmare ended.

When it did, we crawled from the wreckage to discover a sign outside the window that read 'Welcome to Butlin's!' We'd made it, somehow.

My father unhitched the Merc, brought the eldest girls to a dance somewhere and collected 10 bags of chips on the way back to the caravan, before setting off again at midnight to collect the dancers.

He wasn't great at accents, but he enjoyed trying. I remember him speaking in a sort of Dublin accent to the mynah bird in Dublin Zoo, to little avail. He kept saying 'Drawda' when we went to see Oliver Plunkett's head in St Peter's Church in Drogheda, and now, as we headed for the North, he amused himself singing Ruby Murray songs for my mother, complete with Ruby's lovely Belfast swirl.

Tensions were already mounting north of the border. We youngsters didn't fully understand the political landscape of the island, but we guessed something was up when we heard Mam and Dad deciding to pull in north of Dundalk, feed us, reload the fridge and fill the petrol tank before crossing the border. Only when my mother was sure that she had our full and undivided attention did she issue strict instructions to stay quiet at all costs. 'No caffling. We're going into a foreign country. They have different money and the Guards have guns up here. If they hear we're from Cork, we could be shot.'

'This is the best holiday ever,' I thought to myself.

The silence was killing us and was finally broken when, through an open back window, one of the girls shouted, 'Up the IRA!' Before she got to the letter A, my dad had swerved the whole kit and caboodle onto the hard shoulder as a roar was issued from the chasm of his huge chest. 'Jesus Christ Almighty! What are you trying to do to us? I'll crash the car and we'll all get killed and then ye'll have to walk home on yer own! Is that what ye want, hah? Is it?'

Order restored, we cautiously crossed the border and entered Belfast. The field at Finaghy was our target. It was here that thousands of Orangemen and their bands would gather. My mam tried to read the creased Esso roadmap of Ireland with little success as my dad crawled along the red, white and blue kerbs looking for the next clue.

A Royal Ulster Constabulary man with a moustache stepped onto the road and raised his hand in a gesture to halt. He was dressed in a sharp green uniform, with the tip of his peaked cap pulled down to meet the bridge of his nose. As the officer approached the driver's window, my father addressed the man's machine gun in an attempted Belfast accent. Dad's clipped pronunciation and flat vowels were meant to sound like one of the Northern politicians we heard on the telly. He even stuck a whistle on the 'S' to sound like Ian Paisley. 'S(whistle)cuse me there office(whistle)er. Aws thas tha way ta Fawnnahee field?'

The officer was taken aback. He clearly didn't speak Danish, so he asked my father to repeat himself.

'Come again?'

With a shrill whistle, my father began again. 'Ssssshorry offisssher. I ssshaid, ish thash tha way ta Fawnnahyyee faeld?'

It was getting worse. The offisssher looked bemused and pushed his peaked cap well back, as if he was about to scratch his head. However, it was just to give himself clearance to put his head in the driver's window for a good look around. We could clearly see the crown and shamrock on his cap badge. He sniffed the air inside the car as if he could smell trouble. Either that, or he thought my father was smoking cannabis.

'Step out of the car, please.'

I think he only meant my dad, but they were a team so my mam got out too.

In his own good time, the policeman stepped back from the Merc and walked around the entire travelling roadshow. He circled the car and caravan slowly, like a kick-boxer sizing up an opponent. He was as taut as a coiled spring as he peered in the open caravan window at the children peering back from behind the curtains.

A southern registration plate and a dozen children? he must have thought. *Catholics. They have to be.*

We strained to hear from the caravan window as he returned to my father and enquired, 'Where are ye from and where yez headed?'

'Cork,' replied my father sheepishly.

'We just wanted to show the children the Orange parade. We didn't mean any harm,' added my mother apologetically.

The officer took a moment to consider her plea before replying. 'Right, but you'd best park all of this back down in the car-park field and position it up behind the trees. Then come back up to the wall here and stand beside me.'

'Thanks, officer.'

'Sure. Mind how ye go, now,' he replied.

'If we minded how we went, we wouldn't be here at all,' whispered a voice from behind the orange curtain.

My Vocation

In 1968, Fr John O'Sullivan from Castletownbere, a cousin of my mother's, was ordained. I remember it distinctly, because my mother brought me back a present from the ordination in Dublin. It was my very first record, a vinyl 45 of Louis Armstrong singing 'What a Wonderful World'. It was a huge hit that year and my mother loved to hear me sing it.

At the time, Ireland had little political or economic clout, but the fledgling state did pride itself on its worldwide reputation as the land of saints and scholars. We exported our religious communities all over the world as preachers, teachers and nurses. I can well understand how a priest or nun in the family was a source of pride.

My own first cousins Michael and Gerard Creedon from Inchigeelagh were ordained around the same time in All Hallows in Dublin. Michael, like his father, my Uncle John, was a wonderful storyteller. He just loved to talk, and boy, could he laugh. Gerard was quieter, tall and very handsome. Once, when we were all swimming in the river near Inchigeelagh, I overheard two young local women admiring Gerard, who was home on holidays from the seminary. One of them said he would be an awful loss to the village. Gerard wrote poetry and was very philosophical. He once tried to explain the difference between socialism and communism to me. Hardly surprising, then, that he went on to represent the poor of his parish in the Dominican Republic. He also developed an ambulance and pharmacy programme for the people of Bánica before moving to the US, where he became great friends with the family of John F. Kennedy. Indeed, he presided at many of the family weddings and the funeral of Ted Kennedy. His life seemed like one big adventure to me.

Johnny Buckley, a family friend from nearby Graigue in Inchigeelagh, was good friends with Gerard, Michael and the rest of my Uncle John's 14 children. Johnny had also become a priest and was now teaching in Farranferris, the diocesan seminary, not far from our house in Cork City. He had been a regular caller to our home from the time he was a student. Although now an ordained priest – who would eventually become Bishop of Cork and Ross – some of us continued to simply call him 'Johnny'.

My parents had great time for the Buckley family and if Johnny Creedon wasn't around, they'd farm me out to the Buckleys instead, hoping that their gentle ways might rub off on me. I'd be kept busy on the farm and could also call to visit my cousins in the village. At the very least, I'd be off the city streets and attending Mass on Sundays.

Although there was a 20-year age difference between us, I became great old buddies with Johnny Buckley. He would collect me in a groovy Triumph Herald, his pride and joy, and we'd often have a puck-around with the hurleys once we got to Inchigeelagh. The Buckleys were always laughing. They'd knock a bit of sport out of anything and old Mr and Mrs Buckley were very kind to me. They called me 'Cork Johnny'. Their own sons, Neilus, James, Johnny and Paddy, treated me as an unexpected baby brother. They would put me up on one or other of the two giant chestnut horses that spent their working days straining to pull big boulders out of bad land. With Mr Buckley at the reins and helping out with a crowbar to move the stones when required, they worked their way down the mountain, draining and reclaiming land for Neilus to farm in their wake. Mr Buckley would stack the stones to one side, creating small dry-stone walls as he went. On every return to Graigue, I would inspect the work and note the progress.

'How come you have so many walls, Mr Buckley?'

'I dunno,' he'd reply, 'maybe it's because we have so many fields.'

I had to think about that one – and I had plenty of thinking time. Unthinking time too.

Mrs Buckley would send me down the hill with her husband's lunch: a few thick sandwiches and milky tea in a home-made flask, which was an old whiskey bottle, scalded and insulated on the outside by a woollen football sock. On one occasion, James, a champion practical joker, had me memorise a message I was to deliver to his father when I reached him with the flask. I repeated it over and over in my head all the way down the hairpinned boreen until I found Mr Buckley and the horses struggling with an argumentative boulder. Mr Buckley straightened himself and mopped his brow with the back of his hand. I delivered James's telegram exactly as it had been given to me: 'James wants to know where will we sell all the stones when you finish harvesting them? Will it be at Macroom Mart or will we bring them to the fair?'

He smiled at me and looked away for a moment as he considered his own reply. 'Tell James I said he's fired.'

That telegram was easily remembered. It was also delivered exactly as it was given to me and received with much mirth above in the kitchen.

Paddy and James were good hurlers, so I asked them to help me train for the forthcoming donkey derby in Knockraha. They gave me all the tips they could and taught me how to mount a horse without the benefit of a saddle or stirrups. They told me to do press-ups every day. I'd also freewheel, one leg under the crossbar of a huge black High Nelly bicycle, all the way down to the village for hurling training with the Inchigeelagh lads. Then, afterwards, I'd have to push the bike all the way back up to the top of Graigue again. I so wanted to be fit for my one shot at gold and was getting restless for the big day.

ooo

One day, I managed to start the Triumph Herald without anyone seeing me. Whenever Fr Johnny was home for the weekend, he left his car outside the front door of the house with the keys in the ignition. How could I resist? I mean, I had already been in the driver's seat when we push-started the stalled Ford Consul on Coburg Street, and I had spent recent weeks in the back seat of my dad's car while he taught Constance, Geraldine and Vourneen to drive. I knew exactly how to get rolling. 'Check rear-view mirror, ignition on, clutch down, into first gear, right foot on the accelerator, slowly now, release the clutch and slowly apply the accelerator. Keep her lit and keep her between the ditches.' Simple.

Fr Johnny's Triumph was begging for a spin. I slipped in and pulled the driver's seat up close to the steering wheel. I was just about able to see over the dashboard. Ignition, clutch, first, accelerator, clutch up, accelerator down ... and vroom! I roared off out of the yard and down the gravel road towards the first bend in first gear, wondering what to do next.

Fr Johnny and James were outside, having a puck-around that stopped suddenly when they spotted the headless coachman shooting past in Fr Johnny's Triumph Herald. Fortunately, the car stalled just as it was mounting the ditch. Unfortunately, Fr Johnny didn't stall, and as I bailed out the driver's door, he managed to clip me across the backside with the hurley before I escaped through a small gap in the furze and made myself scarce.

I skulked around further up the hill for an hour or more. I pulled the corrugated-iron cover off the well opening, even though I had been warned several times not to go near the well. *I may as well be hung for a sheep as a lamb at this stage.* I passed away the time catching frogs before letting them go again.

I was up with the horses, passing fistfuls of sweet grass in through the six-bar gate to two velvet muzzles, when I heard the call to prayer. Every evening at around dusk, Mrs Buckley would rattle a pot and call anyone who was still outside to come in for the Rosary.

I eventually slipped in amongst the hushed congregation of mother, father and their four adult sons, each kneeling at a kitchen chair for support. I felt like every eye was on me as I pulled a small wooden chair towards myself. If required, my chair could serve a dual purpose – a pew to lean on while I prayed or a defensive barricade to give me a head start on the owner of the stolen car. And so, amidst one stern glance and five sets of raised eyebrows, I joined the chorus.

It was almost dark by the time we had finished the final Glory Be and all the trimmings. One by one we straightened ourselves, groaned and stood up. There was no more said about my misadventure in Fr Johnny's Triumph Herald, other than from James, who just couldn't let the opportunity pass. While dusting the knees of his trousers, he stifled a guffaw before observing with a sigh, 'Well, I suppose even in the Bible it says that Moses himself descended the mountain in Triumph.'

'I'll put on the kettle,' said Mrs Buckley.

Whatever magic is in the Rosary, it truly blesses a household with the gift of divine forgiveness and reconciliation.

ooo

On the way back to Cork with Fr Johnny that Sunday night, I was all talk about becoming a priest. 'I'd love to have a horse like James and go around the country helping people. I could be a cowboy priest.'

'You could. And I'd say you'd make a lovely one too,' he said with a smile. 'But you'd have to knuckle down to the books.'

Whatever about 'the books', I had my mind made up. If I could be a priest, my mother and father would be delighted with me and they'd have to kneel down in front of me for my blessing at my ordination.

Fr Seraphin, a wise old Capuchin with a grey beard and a brown habit like Padre Pio, was a regular visitor to our kitchen for a brandy. Sometimes more than one. He was great craic and he would get fits of the giggles, sometimes so bad that he'd end up trying to catch his breath and spluttering that he'd better go now before he choked on his own jokes. He once told us that hearing a nun's confession was like being stoned to death with popcorn. I asked him if it was hard to live in a monastery. 'Not at all,' he replied. 'Capuchins have the best craic.'

I told Aunty Theresa that I'd like to be a Capuchin cowboy priest, except that I wouldn't be able to ride a big horse like the Buckleys' while wearing the brown habit because people would see my underpants. She agreed with me, but said I'd make a lovely priest all the same. I agreed with her. So, at my mother's request, Fr Johnny Buckley dropped in an application form for the secondary school at St Finbarr's seminary in Farranferris. We filled it out, eventually, and I was called for the entrance exam.

I walked up to the school on my own, but I couldn't find the entrance gate. I met a woman on the footpath and she told me how to get in. I was about twenty minutes late for the first exam and had forgotten to bring a lunch for the break. During the break, I went to the jacks, and while I was standing at the urinal, a big chubby fella with a country accent charged me from behind. He hopped my head off the brick wall. It really hurt.

The maths exam was really hard. I just put in any numbers at all. *You never know*, I thought, *it might just be the right answer.* On the walk home on my own, I was hoping that the big chubby fella with the country accent wasn't waiting to ambush me again. I thought that I had probably failed the entrance exam, but I hoped he wouldn't be in my class in September if I passed.

Because my mother came from Adrigole, which was inside the Kerry diocese, I was also entitled to sit the entrance exam for St Brendan's, a seminary in Killarney. My second-eldest sister, Carol Ann, and her boyfriend drove me there. It was a great day out. Carol Ann was a blonde stunner like Grace Kelly and boys were mad about her. They brought me to the Great Southern Hotel for lunch and I had chicken Maryland for the first time. It was a really posh hotel, with white linen tablecloths and heavy silver cutlery. There was a big sugar cellar on the table and I sprinkled sugar all over my meal, thinking it was salt. When we went into the school, a priest told me that I was the youngest boy sitting the exam. He said that if I passed and became a boarder, as the youngest boy in the whole place I would have the privilege of lighting the school Christmas candle in December. The questions were hard, but the idea of being the boy who lights the Christmas candle was very appealing to me.

Then, in early summer, I sat the entrance exam for Mungret, the Jesuit seminary in Limerick. My dad drove me up to Limerick and we stopped in Croom on the way to buy a pencil, a parer and a rubber because I had forgotten to pack them. The old lady in the shop asked me where I was from. I told her I was from Cork and where I was going, and she said, 'You'll be great. Cork always floats to the top!' Later I told my dad her joke about Cork and we both thought it was a right good one.

Some weeks later, a letter arrived from Mungret wishing me well, but informing my parents that I hadn't made the grade. I was embarrassed when my mother told me. I was disappointed, too, because priests had such great stories and adventures.

My father knew loads of priests and he wasn't one bit shy when he was talking to them. He told me about his friend Canon Deady and the Murphys who lived back west-along in Slieveenroe. 'To say the Murphy place was remote would be no exaggeration. When you turn off the road at Drumtrasna, you'd want a good exhaust pipe to plough the green ridge for over a mile before you'd arrive at "the passage". No car ever drove up that passage without the thorns of a thousand *sceach*s scratching the paintwork on either side of the car.' He went on to tell me that in the winter, after the blackthorn and hawthorn had been given a good tight crew cut, a tidy donkey and cart could negotiate that little boreen, but otherwise the passage was, in fact, unpassable.

I knew the place. There wasn't a farmyard as such, not in the modern concrete sense anyway, just the limestone rock upon which the cottage sat. The rock was bare and had been polished by over a century of wheel, foot and hoof.

As is often the case with people in remote places, words were equally remote. The chatter of townies was a foreign language to the Murphys. Instead their language, like their land, was sparse and rough.

There was no mirror in the house. It showed. Mrs Murphy would arrive at the door fousterin' and pushing back a big mop of hair that was once styled in a bun. 'Chrisht, I'm like a pookie pile ... the Wreck of the Hesperus,' she'd say.

Everybody was fond of the Murphys, but they were loud and uncouth betimes. The schoolmaster used to say the Murphys didn't have a couth between them. Young Mags Murphy disgraced him when Canon Deady came to examine the children for Holy Communion. The Canon went through the entire ceremony, rehearsing and testing the children to make sure they understood their faith. He had worked his way towards the back of the class.

'What's your name, girleen?'

'Mags Murphy, Canon.'

'Good girl, Mags. Will you say the Our Father for me?'

'Our Father,' she began, 'who art above in heaven. Hollow be thy name, as it is above in heaven. Blessed are these, eh ... gifts.'

'Hold on, child. Do you know it at all?'

'N-n-no, Father.'

'That's OK,' he encouraged her, 'just say the Hail Mary for us so.'

'Holy Mary, above in heaven. Blessed be the fruit of thy loom and thou too Jesus ...'

'Hold on a while, do you know that one either?'

'No, Father.'

'Do you know any old prayer at all?'

'Well, my mother do say the grace after meals.'

'Go on so. Say that for us,' he replied with a sigh of relief.

'Oh God ...' she began out loud, as if about to deliver a speech, 'I'll busht!' she concluded.

And that was it, her mother's grace after meals in its entirety: 'Oh God, I'll busht.'

'In ways, I suppose it's as good a grace after meals as any other,' said my father, 'so Canon Deady gave her the go-ahead and she made her First Holy Communion.'

Some years later, when Canon Deady announced that the Murphys would be hosting the next Stations, a quiet 'Christ!' rippled through the congregation.

The Stations, a custom dating from penal times when the saying of Mass was outlawed and priests were routinely hunted, requires a host family. Each household in turn would be expected to host a morning Mass and breakfast for priest and parish. The days leading up to the Stations were all go. Action stations, you could say. There was starched linen and flowers for the altar table, a coat of whitewash for the cottage exterior, a lick of paint for the inside and as hearty a breakfast for the guests as the household could muster.

Fasting from the night before, all the neighbours would file in, blessing themselves with holy water from the little font on the wall just inside the front door. The host would be complimented on the fresh paintwork and the fine spread-in-waiting on the kitchen table.

In hushed tones, older women and guests of honour would be ushered into the parlour, or 'the room', as many households referred to it. 'Slip away in there for yourself, Mrs Twomey. There's an empty chair there beside Hannah.'

After Mass, the priest would come back up from 'the room' and greet the neighbours who had been standing in the kitchen, leaning towards the sound of the sacrament being celebrated below in the room. On this occasion, as soon as the Canon concluded his meet and greet, he was steered towards the seat of honour: an armchair by the fire.

Everyone agreed that it had all gone really well and that the Murphys had put on a spread that far exceeded their circumstances and the expectations of the parish.

Old Mrs O'Driscoll, who had brought the starched tablecloths and some extra cutlery, was fousterin' around between the kitchen and the parlour. She dispatched young Mags with a plate of ham and hardboiled eggs, two cuts of brown bread and a lump of butter on the side.

'Here you are, Canon,' offered Mags. 'There's plenty more bread there, but mind the butter, 'tis as soft as shite.'

Canon Deady recoiled in disbelief and the congregation gasped. But, quick as a wink, Mags's mother was in, mid-gasp, to retrieve the situation.

'Whist, Mags, will you shut up?!' she reprimanded her daughter, as she turned to the priest to apologise. 'Never mind her, Canon, she's as ignorant as me arse!'

Priests had so much fun. I couldn't wait to be one.

The Formica Bar

As you entered the Formica Bar on Ship Street, you passed under a sign that read, 'Early house. Licensed to sell beers, wines and spirits. The proprietor reserves the right of admission.'

Indeed, the proprietor was the only thing reserved about the place. He managed to keep a formal distance from the customers who spent hours perched opposite him. Although he had once studied to become a pharmacist, the owner, Albert Barry, discovered far too late in life that destiny had cheated him. Somehow, he had ended up behind his father's bar counter, dispensing painkillers by the pint to the same drunks his father had hated before him. However, the bar provided a good income and there was a steady procession of stool pigeons ready to take a perch as soon as one of the older lads died and fell off.

Once, on my way to school at about half past eight on a weekday morning, through the small window in the bar from which tobacco smoke whooshed, I heard a man inside sneeze. Without missing a beat, Mr Barry's muffled bellow followed: 'Get out! And you can take your germs with you! You're barred! Get out!'

I knew he wasn't talking to me. He was always nice to me; it was the men he hated.

A schoolteacher called Mr Coakley, a great customer, once got the door for quietly reading a book while drinking his lunch. I saw it with my own two eyes. Mr Barry inhaled deeply, summoning up that dismissive whine favoured by the Cork middle classes, and pronounced judgement with a well-worn sigh. 'OK, Mr Coakley, let's be having you. The Central Library is below on the Grand Parade. Off with you now, and you can bring your book with you. Good man. Bye-bye now and don't be coming back. Thank you.'

Mr Barry gave me some of the best beer mats in my collection. I had three different Beamish ones from the brewery just down the street, a Double Diamond, a Caffrey's, a Celebration Ale and a Macardle's, which Mr Barry told me you could only get in Dundalk up by Northern Ireland. I also had one for Holsten Pils, which he said was given to him by a Nazi tank driver who was in the bar one night.

Every time I ran away from home, it was to the Formica I'd go. Mr Barry would always give me a glass of raza. Balanced on my high stool, I'd watch down the line as the beer went down and the egos came out to play.

Three Benson & Hedges ashtrays were spread out evenly along the Formica countertop and six leatherette high stools stood to attention outside. A clock with a colourful toucan and a caption that declared 'Always Time for a Guinness' was kept 10 minutes closer to closing time than the real time, and a parade of glazed Gaelic Games figurines lined out across the shelf above the optics. Sponsored by Player's No. 6 cigarettes, each player wore his county colours. I knew them all. The easiest county to recognise was Kilkenny with the black-and-amber striped jersey. The Down footballer looked classy, a bit like an English soccer player with his red-and-black trims and black knicks. But my favourite was the Cork player sporting the red and white of Cork, or 'de ole blood 'n' bandage' as Cider Joe, an oul' fella who did most of his drinking in the morning, always called it. I'd have loved to own a set of those figurines.

A giant mirror ran along the back wall behind the counter so that Mr Barry could keep an eye on his clientele in the same way as Mr Moriarty the barber could. The ceiling was held together by woodchip wallpaper and the nicotine resin of a million cigarettes. There was a row of cracks along the plaster that held the red velvet wall lights, most of them without a bulb. Another row of cracks ran along the high stools: men's arses peeping above their trouser belts, as if instructed to 'watch me back' to see who might be passing in, while the lad beside them was passing out. It seemed no one, Mr Barry or the men outside the counter, ever looked at themselves in the mirror. They were all too busy watching 'the other fuckers', as they called each other.

The lounge was down the other end of the bar and had carpet for the women. The carpet was sticky to walk on and smelled of Glade air freshener. The toilet was in a once-whitewashed shed out in the concrete yard. The frosted window was covered in webs and half-eaten flies. The three urinals usually had a fistful of small yellow urinal blocks in them at various stages of disintegration. The walls were stained with dried stout spits, and someone had written 'Shamrock Rovers Bootboys Rule' on the door. I hated using it.

Cork folk singer Jimmy Crowley described the Formica Bar as the kind of place where they'd cut your throat behind your back, and if you weren't careful, they'd even stab you in the back, right in front of your face. It was a world of sarcasm and contradictions.

One day after school, I dropped in for a drink.

Chuck Mulrooney, an American with an Irish name, was on his usual perch by the phone. He had left his family in South Carolina and moved to Ireland because, he reckoned, American bars were boring. He kept talking about 'the craic', even when no one was listening.

Mulrooney claimed he could never find the time to delve any deeper into his family tree, so he would just repeat the same old calling card to any newcomer: 'My great-grandfather was a notorious landlord with an enormous appetite for claret, servant girls and money,' he'd chortle. 'The family got the ole one-way ticket to the States during the Famine. My grandfather was only five years old at the time and didn't want to leave old Ireland. But hey, it was either that or marry the girl,' he'd chuckle to himself, snorting into his pint.

One time, as he was saying it, Cider Joe dismissed Mulrooney's claims with 'Yeah, and my grandmother was a volunteer in 1916.'

'Really? Cumann na mBan?' Mulrooney enquired.

'No, Meals on Wheels,' says Cider Joe.

Mulrooney would snort into his pint again. His own story never went beyond the 'marry the girl' bit, so I had no idea what he was on about. I didn't really like Mulrooney, I felt sorry for him, but I loved listening to his accent.

Above his head and around the bar counter, the flies circled as he droned on.

Mr Barry coughed and cleared his throat, a signal to those who had any sense to shut up because the man with the right to refuse admission was about to speak.

'There are two kinds of fly, the bluebottle and the house fly.' The Formica had plenty of both, living and dead, especially on the windowsill behind the window seat, where a tiny old man known as 'the Ould Soldier' spent much of the afternoon asleep.

'The bluebottle has some disgusting habits. It lands on any shit that's available,' Mr Barry declared while eyeballing Mulrooney. 'He samples it with the taste buds under his feet, then when he finishes absorbing enough of it, he moves on and spreads it wherever he goes: countertops, church altars, babies' bottles. It's all the same to him, as long as he's spreading shit.'

Mr Barry mounted a footstool, its padded velvet seat polished by the arses of dead men and decades of farts and spilt drinks, and continued.

'Now, the house fly, by comparison, is a far more annoying but patently less deadly member of the species,' he said as he unfurled the sticky fly paper. 'Unlike the bluebottle, who will depart a premises at the first invitation to do so, the house fly will circle a bulb endlessly, pursuing one of its own. Try as one might, there's no clearing them.'

Sure enough, two flies were circling the 60-watt bulb in their own Battle of Britain.

The Ould Soldier woke up, shell-shocked, and immediately Mulrooney called him a pint of Beamish. He always did that to stop people leaving. Even me. 'Here, give the kid a pack of potato chips,' he'd say, pointing at the Tayto tin behind the counter. I couldn't resist, even though I knew I'd be late and Mam would threaten to farm me out or send me to boarding school.

As Mr Barry plonked a fresh pint of stout on the bar counter for the Ould Soldier, Mulrooney piped up. 'I say, bartender, I'm afraid we have a little conundrum. I believe I owe you four shillings for this fine pint. However, I find I'm sixpence short of the required four shillings.' Then, nodding in the direction of myself and Cider Joe, he continued. 'So, perhaps one of these kind gentlemen can furnish me with the aforementioned sixpence, or perhaps you might simply waive the discrepancy?'

Even I knew this stunt was out of order and that Mulrooney had pushed his welcome right to the cliff edge. Cider Joe and myself braced ourselves as the 'bartender' sauntered back over to 'Dead Man Sitting' at the counter.

Taking his time, Mr Barry rested his two elbows on the counter directly in front of the Yank and leaned in till he was nose to nose with the customer. Cider Joe and myself looked away and the Ould Soldier just looked around him, confused as usual.

Staring Mulrooney straight in the eye, the proprietor whispered menacingly, 'In this part of the world, Mr Mulrooney, we have a solution for such conundrums.' And, lowering his head until his lips were level with the rim of Mulrooney's glass, he casually slugged the creamy head until he had swallowed about an eighth of the pint in one go.

'Now, there you go, Mulrooney. Three and sixpence will do ya,' he pronounced while sweeping the coins off the Formica countertop.

Later, with the status quo restored, Cider Joe pointed at the glazed football figurines and continued testing my knowledge of the county colours. Then we moved on to county car-registration numbers.

'Cork reg plates end in …?'

'PI and ZF,' I replied.

'Correct. Waterford?'

'KI.'

'Kerry?'

'IN.'

Mr Barry examined the scene before him. Cider Joe with his tortured face in the middle, me full of enthusiasm on the high stool to his left and a chastened Mulrooney on his right looking into his pint. The proprietor passed judgement as only he could and, addressing Cider Joe, declared, 'Look at you, you're like Christ himself on the cross … and I s'pose that's the good thief there on yer left and the quare thief on yer right, huh?'

We were distracted by the sound of something rattling. It was Mulrooney's glasses falling to the floor, followed by Mulrooney.

'Christ!' said Mr Barry, as he stopped mid-pour. 'Are you all right there, Chuck?'

By the sound of the heavy thump with which he landed on the floorboards, we knew he wasn't all right. Also, no one ever called Mulrooney 'Chuck', so I knew he was in trouble, even though his eyes were open.

Mr Barry had one look and went straight to the coin box. He dialled 999 but he didn't insert a coin, so I knew it was an emergency – the call was free if someone was dead or dying. Mulrooney was dead. Cider Joe put a coat on top of him, probably to keep him warm and to keep the flies off him.

It was the first time I had seen a dead man.

'You'd better go home now, John,' said Mr Barry. And then, addressing his two remaining customers, he added, 'The Guards will be here in a minute, does anyone want a quick pint there? Because I'll be closing up now shortly.'

I downed my raza and made for the door. Like an eejit, I ran straight home and told Mam and Dad what I had just witnessed. I thought they would have been amazed to hear that I saw Mulrooney dead, but they were cross with me for being in a bar again after I'd promised I'd stop. Later, I heard my dad talking to my mother about me again.

'He's safer below in Lackenroe with Johnny than he is here at home, but Jesus, we'll have to get him in someplace after the summer or 'tis himself will be dead, not Mulrooney. I hope to God he'll get in someplace.'

The Donkey Derby

I was in the kitchen when my mother got the letter from St Finbarr's seminary in Farranferris. As she read it, I read her expression. She sighed, nodded to herself as if to say, 'I might have guessed,' and folded the letter. When she put it into my father's top drawer, I knew ... I didn't need to hear my father tut and throw his eyes up to heaven to have it confirmed. I just knew. I thought of the big country boy who had hopped my head off the jacks wall and part of me was relieved to be rejected. The rest of me was relieved to be farmed out again that weekend.

Johnny called on his way home from work to collect me and the waste. 'Well, are you ready for Sunday?'

I shrugged. 'I dunno. Will there be many people there?'

'Thousands.'

'Who are the other jockeys?'

'I don't know yet, but Young Harrington from over the road is definitely riding.'

'Young Harrington? But he's about twenty!'

'Sure I know, but what harm, his legs are too long to be a jockey.'

When we arrived in Lackenroe, there was no sign of Mick, so I guessed that he was already in the haggard with Mrs Manley waiting to feed the pigs. Johnny backed in the car and it was straight to work. The sows knew what was coming. They snorted and squealed and jostled for position, but Mick, who would normally be running rings around me with excitement, was lying in the hay shed and just gave his tail a wag to say hello. I patted his curly head and asked what was wrong with him.

'Erra, poor ole Mickeen is off colour, aren't you, pet?' Mrs Manley cooed sympathetically as she scratched him under the chin. 'You are, you poor divil. Wind from over-eating, like myself,' she chuckled. 'Johnny will bring you to the vet on Monday if you're not right.'

Johnny pulled the slop buckets out of the boot of the car and heaved them up onto the wall above the feeding troughs. Mrs Manley threw a few fistfuls of pig ration in on top of the eggshells, cabbage leaves and potato skins. 'Here you are, Fatty Arbuckle, you're dining with the Creedons again tonight,' she chuckled.

Later, as we rinsed out the buckets, I told Mrs Manley about the letter my mother got about me and she listened. Mick listened too.

'It's not that I want to be troublesome, I'm just no good at anything. I came last in sums again and Brother O'Hare said I was a disgrace. My mother says I'm arch. I even scored a goal against my own team in hurling and now I'm going to make a fool of myself again in the donkey derby.'

'Yerra, the divil fire 'em all,' was the only consolation she could offer.

I was awake half the night. I must have fallen asleep for a while because I dreamt I was in the Formica Bar and that Mulrooney was still alive. Then he was in a donkey race, but he was dead and tied onto the donkey and he was flopping all over the place like the scarecrow in *The Wizard of Oz*.

It was bright and I was awake for a long time before I heard the 'krrrrrraaannggg' as the clockwork hammer between the two little bells on top of Johnny's alarm clock went off like a machine gun. I really, really didn't want to get up.

The gnawing in my stomach felt like hunger pangs, but I couldn't eat the fry for breakfast.

We drove down towards the crossroads for Knockraha, Glenville and Glanmire. We were hardly on the road a minute or two when Johnny turned left through an open gate and into a freshly mown meadow. There were four or five other cars already there and a white Cortina pulling a horsebox was right on our tail. Johnny backed the Morris Minor onto the grassy bank and parked her beside the last car in the row. There was no bunting like you might get at a carnival, but the course looked very big and impressive. About the same size as Croke Park, I'd say. There were no rails, but a rope ran around the centre to create an oval-shaped, football-pitch-sized safe space inside it and a racecourse around it. There was a small incline on the way out the course that served as a dip on the way back down towards the start and finish line.

We stayed in the car while Johnny drove the race plan into my head one more time. I had it all off by heart, but I knew my real challenge would be driving it into Rosie's thick skull. 'The race is counterclockwise, so lean herself into the left at all times, but don't fall off. At the starting line, keep her on a tight rein with her head well up. As soon as you see the marshal raise the flag, start roaring at her like the place is on fire but hold her back. Then, the very second you see the marshal start to move his shoulder, drive your heels good and hard into her sides, give the reins a bit of slack, but for God's sake ... are you listening to me now?'

'I am.'

'For the love of Christ, do ... not ... fall ... off.'

'I'll do my best.'

'I'm not asking you to do your best. I'm telling you not to fall off! Do you hear me?'

'I do.'

By now, the hollow in my stomach was the size of a basketball.

We didn't have a horsebox, so Mrs Manley had walked Rosie down earlier and they were both waiting for me. The huddle of men and boys were standing in a circle, smoking and laughing away for themselves.

Mrs Manley stood apart under a flowering whitethorn *sceach*, out of the way of the men and shaded from the burning sun. Rosie looked beautiful. Mrs Manley had put a brightly coloured folded blanket across her back. No saddles were allowed but she was still dressed for the occasion. And Rosie knew it was an occasion. Although wearing blinkers, she knew full well there was something up. Her surroundings were unusual and her two big fluffy ears twitched backwards and forwards independent of each other, adjusting to the sounds of the voices. She recognised my voice and gave her harness a good jingle and shook her head vigorously, as if getting ready for something big that was just about to happen.

I felt a little braver when I saw Rosie had showed up and was good to go. 'She's mad for action, lads,' Mrs Manley said encouragingly. 'She had a good feed of the right grub earlier and her form is right.'

A small man wearing a flat cap and a long tan shop coat shouted, 'Good luck, lads!' over his shoulder at nobody in particular, then he headed out the course carrying a Ballinahina Dairy milk crate in one hand and a rolled-up flag in the other. 'That's the starter,' said Johnny, 'and that's the clerk of the course over there talking to the elderly man in the bowler hat. He's the judge.'

I sneaked a look at them and recognised the clerk of the course as Mr Harrington, Young Harrington's father. He was a nice man and was probably very fair. I didn't know the judge, but he smiled at me and he was probably fair as well, or else he wouldn't be a judge.

I was hoping I might see Louie Angelini, but there were no bookies around. Even so, Johnny said big money would be changing hands 'unknownst to us'.

The crowd was small too. I only counted about fourteen people, including the handful that stayed in their cars like they always did at Glounthaune football matches when it was raining. They all flashed their headlamps and blew their horns if there was a score. But I definitely saw some kids coming in the gate as the clerk of the course called all runners and riders to come forward.

I already knew Young Harrington, so I nodded hello to him when our eyes met.

'How're you and how're they all in Cork?' he shouted.

'Grand,' says I.

He didn't seem one bit nervous. I was. Why wouldn't I be? I mean, Young Harrington lived on a farm and had a moustache an' all.

I didn't really know the other two jockeys, but I recognised them from outside the Sugarloaf shop. It was Greasy Deasy who ran the petrol pumps and a saucy fella from Knockraha.

The clerk of the course summoned us. 'Wait for the flag. Three times around the course. No striking an opponent or their animal. Any jockey falling off during the race shall be permitted to remount without disqualification, provided the donkey re-enters the race at the same point at which the fall occurred. It's first over the line. Winner takes all. So bless yourselves now and mount up.'

We did.

The starter was away out the course, standing on the blue milk crate. He raised the green flag and I turned Rosie towards the starting line. We all shuffled towards the starting tape – a length of twine held at either end by two men leaning backwards as if they were trying to stretch it.

'Steady! Steady, Rosie,' I growled nice and quietly, as Young Harrington on the big old donkey beside me leaned into us. Rosie lined up perfectly but the saucy fella from the Sugarloaf was having difficulty. He was pulling too hard with his right hand and had the poor eejit of a donkey confused and turning round and round on the spot.

Eventually, the four riders were all in a row and under starter's orders. I leaned back and my hands scuttled up along the reins to tighten my grip and shorten the slack. Rosie knew well what was coming and the second the starter looked like he was going to drop the green flag, I began to gee her up with a rocking movement of my hips, while keeping the reins tight and her head up. There was no time for nerves: I had a job to do now.

The flag was halfway through its downward arc when the starting tape dropped and Rosie shot off like the human cannonball. We were out in front, but I dared not look over my shoulder to check the others in case I fell off. As we rounded the first bend, I chanced a glance across the course to my left and confirmed that the saucy fella who had been going around in circles was still at it, away back the course. But I could hear the other two roaring instructions just behind me, and by the sound of it Young Harrington was right on my donkey's tail.

As we completed the first lap and clattered past the spectators, I could hear Mrs Manley above the roar of the crowd. 'Drive on, Rosie, the best dunkey in the whole of Glounthaune!' Some of the people who had stayed in their cars out of the sun flashed their headlamps in silent applause.

It was now a three-donkey race and we were still bunched coming down the dip towards the crowd.

'Reins and mane!' roared Johnny as we shot past.

'The divil fire 'em all! Drive on!' screeched Mrs Manley like a banshee.

'Winner takes all!' shouted Greasy Deasy's mother, Mrs Deasy.

This was like one of my dreams. I couldn't make sense of all the different things that were going on at the same time, but I had to hang on.

'I'm not going to win this,' I told myself, 'but at all costs, do ... not ... fall ... off!'

Coming down the dip for a second time, Greasy Deasy's donkey stumbled on an old ploughing ridge and fell.

'Pride before a fall, greaseball!' shouted Young Harrington.

'Fuck you!' shouted Greasy at Young Harrington and at his own donkey, who was limping. It was down to a two-donkey race.

Rosie stopped. That was it. She just stopped. Why? Who knows? Donkeys are like that. Young Harrington trotted past us.

I would never, ever use a sally rod on a donkey, but you'd think she'd feel me kicking my heels into her hide. No, like a daisy in a bull's mouth, she hardly even noticed. I roared at her, but she was pure Bodhar Uí Laoighre. I slapped her rump, shook the reins, and rocked my hips. Nothing. I sat there looking at Young Harrington a few hundred yards from home and I just didn't know what to do. So I did what Mrs Manley would do. I spoke nicely to Rosie.

I brought my nose tip to tip with the point of her big furry ear and sighed, 'Aw, c'mon, Rosie girl. Pleeeease c'mon. Don't let us all down. Just do it for Johnny and Mrs Manley. C'mon, Rosie girl. Do it for Seán Dunphy ... do it for your own mam.'

I was hoping for a reaction, but she took her time about it. She must have been considering what I had just said. Well, the next thing, Rosie shook herself and nearly shook me off her back. She started into a bit of a trot, like a lady in high heels. Then she broke into a gallop, but we were still in second place with nearly a lap to go. Deasy had remounted but he was way back the course, so we could hardly come last, but Young Harrington was well ahead and was full tilt for the finish line. I could hear the spectators shouting him on and the car horns honking on the grassy bank.

Rosie took a wobble coming down the dip and I slipped to my left, but she kept going. The downward pressure of my weight was pulling Rosie's head down and in towards the left. I managed to release the reins or else I'd have turned her hard left into the ropes with me. Life was whizzing past my left ear as I gripped Rosie's mane in a white-knuckle ride to rival the Ballybunion Ghost Train. I just couldn't right myself and continued on my downward slide until I had swung completely underneath, with my legs wrapped around the base of her neck and my two arms around her upper neck, fists gripping that ridge of coarse donkey hair that passes as a mane. I was hanging upside down, looking up at her flared nostrils. I could see a look of pure madness in her big glassy eyes inside the blinkers, and she was dribbling froth on top of my hair. My weight had her head lowered to almost grazing height, but onwards she strove at walking pace.

And that's how we wobbled down the home straight and over the finish line.

I could hear the people roaring and the cars honking for Young Harrington, but at least we had finished the race and I did … not … fall … off.

Mrs Manley was first up to us, running. 'Ringadora! You bate the lot of 'em.'

Johnny was right behind her, breathless like there was something wrong. 'Good man yourself. Well done, champ!'

I tried to correct him. 'Young Harrington hammered me. I'm sorry about that, Johnny, but I s'pose at least we kept going anyway.'

'Kept going? You won!'

'Huh?'

'You won! Young Harrington is away back up the field. Look!'

'Huh?'

'The racket from all the bloody car horns spooked his donkey and she took off.'

'What?'

'She ran away with him. While you were looking into Rosie's mouth, Harrington's donkey took off back the way she came! You've won the cup, you divil!'

I actually had. I wasn't sure how or why, but I had just won the Glounthaune Donkey Derby Perpetual Trophy.

The judge in the bowler hat presented me with the trophy, Mrs Deasy took my photograph, and I shook hands with the other three jockeys. Everybody who was there clapped, and the people who weren't there heard about it later when Johnny drove Mrs Manley and myself over to use the phone in the Sugarloaf and to buy lemonade and Taytos and a Gateaux Swiss Roll.

'And a bag of carrots!' says I from the back seat.

'Don't mind yer oul' carrots,' growled Mrs Manley from the passenger seat. 'Rosie will have sugary cake like the rest of us.'

I went straight to the phone in the side hall in the Sugarloaf. When I heard Rosaleen's voice say, 'Hello, 20319?', I pressed button A and said, ''Tis me. We won. Will you tell Mam and Dad?'

'I will, of course, that's brilliant! Will you need Dad to go down and collect you?'

'No, Johnny is going to drop me off on his way into work on Monday morning. I'll have the trophy with me.'

'That's fantastic news. I'll tell everyone.'

'Do. And tell the customers in the shop too. Thanks, Rosaleen. I love you.'

'Love you too, Johnny Woggles.'

On the way back to Lackenroe, I asked Johnny if we would get a copy of the photograph of me with the trophy 'in case I run into Sullivan, who never believes me about anything. When he says "Where's the proof?" I'll just show him the photograph.' Johnny said he'd ask.

I knew well that it would be better not to give Rosie any of the Swiss roll, but I still went down to the donkey house after the grub and gave all three donkeys – Rosie, Deirdre and Philip the foal – a good armful of hay and a few chunks of chopped apple and topped up their water. I kept patting Rosie's back and telling her that I was just so grateful for what she had done that day. I kept calling her 'champ' for ages, the way Johnny called me 'champ' when we won.

Mick was still out of sorts, but he wagged his tail a little when I said, 'Look, Mick, the trophy. We won.'

Johnny made a bed near the fireplace for Mick from a cardboard box and an old pair of curtains. He assured me that Mick would be fine in the morning and that we would bring him to the vet on the way to Cork if he wasn't perfect.

I couldn't wait to get home to Cork, so I packed up all my stuff and, as I carefully wrapped the trophy in old newspaper, I saw a grubby, dog-eared sticker on the underside of the base: 'Paid. To be collected by Mr J. Creedon.' Mrs Manley saw me reading it and quickly peeled it off and stuck it in her apron pocket. 'How well they knew you'd be the winner, hah?'

'What? Oh yeah,' I replied. 'It's amazing, Mrs Manley. My mam and dad won't believe I won something. They'll be delighted when they see me coming home with the trophy.'

'They will, Johnny boy,' said Mrs Manley. 'There'll be bonfires blazing for you at every crossroads from here to Cork!'

Riding off into the Sunset

The following morning, I bounced out of bed and ran into the kitchen to check on Mick. He was still in the box. I took one furtive look and recoiled in denial. No way.

'Quick, Johnny. Come quick!' I screamed.

He was up and into the kitchen in a flash, wearing his long johns and a long face.

'Mick is a mother,' I announced.

'What?'

'Mick is a mam. He's after having pups.'

I counted them. Sure enough, four black and tan puppies, all with their eyes closed, snuggling up to their mother, Mick.

'Well, I never,' declared Johnny.

'And you told me that some male dogs do their pooley sitting down.'

'They do,' he insisted.

If ever I wished Johnny's house had a phone, it was that morning.

About twenty minutes later, Mrs Manley announced her arrival for the milking with a knock on the door, before lifting the latch and arriving in, talking to herself. '... if we don't make a start soon. How are the two Johnnys and how's the patient this morn–?' She stopped in her tracks, before gasping incredulously. 'Is it joking me ye are, is it?'

'No, Mrs Manley. It's true.'

'My God, that bates all,' she said, shaking her head. 'The dog that couldn't lay an egg, hah? By Christ, he must have laid dem four during the night,' she laughed.

'Don't mind your old "he",' said Johnny in mock reprimand. '"Tis "she" from now on.'

'Will we have to change his name, so?' I wondered aloud.

We all paused for a split second to consider the matter, before Mrs Manley announced, 'Michelle!' She said it with a real posh accent, like she was introducing the Queen of England.

A few moments later we were all out in the cow shed, milking away, a cow each, wisecracking to each other from below the cows and above the racket as streams of milk pelted the galvanised buckets.

'Can we change Teresa McGonagle's name to Thomas McGonagle for the craic?' I shouted.

'Yerra, we can,' roared Johnny.

'Whatever else ye do, ye'd better count those pups again in case ye got that wrong too!' screeched Mrs Manley. 'And check that they're actually pups and not chicks. Jesus wept!' she roared, laughing at her own joke.

'This is probably the best twenty-four hours in my whole life since I was born,' I announced. 'I'm now a champion jockey and a sort of a stepfather to the four pups, I s'pose.'

'You are,' Johnny confirmed. 'You're on the crest of a wave, champ!' he added, putting the seal on it.

ooo

However, as sure as night follows day, the crest of a wave is followed by a trough. By bedtime I had a lump in my throat. I couldn't bear to leave Mick and the pups, and I wasn't sure anymore about becoming a priest or going to any boarding school that would take me. I just wanted to stay in Lackenroe with Johnny and Mrs Manley and Mick and the pups and everyone else.

When I got home from Glounthaune, I told everybody the great news about Rosie and Mick and myself. Marie-Thérèse whispered to me that there was even more news. A letter had arrived from St Brendan's seminary in Killarney. I was in.

Deep down, I had been relieved that the other two schools had said no and was petrified that St Brendan's might say yes. But, as the youngest boarder in the school, at least I'd be allowed to light the school candle at Christmas. I tried to focus on that part of the deal and the fact that my parents now finally knew that I really had done my best at the entrance exam.

I told my mother that I'd probably miss her a lot. But she said, 'Don't be worrying about that because the school brochure said that boys can use the phone once they have permission from the Dean.' She promised she'd give me a note asking that I be allowed to call home and that she would also give me a bag of sixpences for the phone.

Anyway, I was 11 years old now. It was time to be a man and I only had eight weeks to prepare, so I wrote out my own packing list:

Buy a pair of pyjamas
Bring Glounthaune Donkey Derby Perpetual Trophy
Hurley
Orange bell-bottoms
Football boots
Cork Hibs jersey
Sweets
New copybooks
Geometry set

I thought about bringing Seán Bunny, but I knew they'd only laugh at me and I had kind of grown out of him anyway, so he went into the box of Christmas decorations in the attic. At least I'd know where to find him at Christmas, when I'd next be home.

ooo

The rest of that summer saw me back and forth to Glounthaune. Johnny used to joke that I would have to call down more often because the women had him outnumbered. 'Between Mrs Manley and Michelle and Teresa McGonagle, I haven't a hope.'

Mrs Manley was still getting a kick out of Mick's surprise family. Every time she saw him she'd say something like 'Ringadora! I wouldn't doubt you, Mickeen! All the years I said you couldn't even lay an egg, hah? Well, the divil fire dem curls of yours, we thought you were a little maneen and all along 'twas a lady we had, hah?'

We never got used to calling Mick 'Michelle', so we just kept calling her Mick.

On my last visit, Johnny said that, for the craic, I should ask Louie Angelini if, as Mick's original owner and grandfather to the pups, he'd like to take one of them. I never did.

I went out to the haggard to say goodbye to Mrs Manley. We stood there looking at each other. Eventually, she took my hand in hers ... and shook it. 'Good luck with everything,' she whispered. Then she said she'd better run off because she thought she left the kettle boiling below in the house.

Johnny shook my hand too, even though he would be driving me back to Cork later.

ooo

I spent the morning of my departure to St Brendan's rooting around under the back stairs looking for a hurley. I was always nervous looking under the stairs. It was full of spiders and if a rat ever got into the house from McKenzie's, it would be in there he'd probably go.

All I could see was old paint tins, a yard brush and a USA biscuit tin with fuses and batteries and old rusty bolts, nails and screws that never actually came in handy. I sensed someone standing behind me.

'What are you looking for? Is it the sewer rods?' he chuckled.

'Naw, a hurley, Dad.'

'Erra, you'll need no hurley in Kerry. 'Tis all football in the Kingdom. Take the boots. Your dear old dad kicked a few points with them in his day.'

Yeah, and my grandfather too, I thought to myself. They were ancient, like something Christy Ring wore in all those old black-and-white photographs in the Formica Bar.

Because my older brother Don never played football before me, they had been under the stairs since my dad literally 'hung up his boots' when he got married in 1943. They had been ageing in the darkness for 27 years. The two-tone brown and tan ankle-high boots had dried up like the skin of a bog body; they were hard as a rock with soles and studs like timber. But they were my dad's and he was giving them to me. I couldn't hurt his feelings and we weren't made of money, so I said, 'Thanks a million, Dad. I'll mind them.'

He shifted awkwardly and, turning away, he rummaged in his money pocket – the front right. The driver's seat, I called it. Squinting downwards like a cattleman at a fair, he checked he had the right amount.

I was hoping he would give me a half-crown, like he did the day we went to Ballybunion, but this was no half-crown. This was a ten-bob note.

He said something about not losing it, for Christ's sake. It was love at first sight. My first-ever paper money and probably the most beautiful note of them all. It was a powerful orange colour set against a pale green wash, with a portrait painting of Lady Lavery by her husband, Sir John Lavery, on it. In bold capitals, it declared, 'THE CENTRAL BANK OF IRELAND, LEGAL TENDER NOTE'. All kinds of intricate Celtic details were woven into the design. *That's to stop robbers making their own money*, I thought to myself.

Lady Lavery looked just like my mother did when she was a young girl in Adrigole. She had a light shawl draped loosely over a full head of thick, dark hair. Her beautiful, dainty face looked out at me, as if she was worried about me or something.

My blossoming love affair with Lady Lavery was interrupted by Dad's voice. 'That's a good deal more than I got when I was heading off to school, so pin it into your pocket. They'll probably have a tuck shop below, so you won't be short of an oul' Trigger bar, or whatever ye call 'em. But don't be stuck. If you run short, just drop me a line and at the end of the letter put "Funds are low". I'll know what that means. Good man. You'll be fine.' He rubbed my back and ran for work.

My sisters were all fussing around me and I gave them all a big hug. We were always great huggers. Rosaleen and Marie-Thérèse were going back to their boarding school in the morning and had their maroon uniforms hanging up. Marie-Thérèse gave me a piece of paper. It read, 'Marie-Thérèse Creedon, Saint Aloysius, Main Street, Carrigtwohill, Co. Cork. Ad Jesum per Mariam.' I put it in my pocket and we promised that we'd write to one another. We did. For years.

Johnny Creedon called to collect the waste a bit earlier that week so he could say goodbye again before I was gone. He was chatting away to Miss Healy in the shop about his plans to build a bungalow in Lackenroe when I arrived downstairs with my suitcase.

'Here comes the scholar!' he announced. 'Off to the Kingdom. Don't be taking any notice of those Kerry lads now, do you hear me?'

'I do.'

'They have high notions of themselves, like the goats in Kerry.'

We both laughed, because he used to always say the same thing about Teresa McGonagle, the cow that broke our hearts.

'I'm not great for the letter-writing, so I said I'd bring you this.' He reached into his inside pocket and slipped me a photograph of Mr Harrington and the judge presenting me with the cup at the donkey derby. You could just see Mrs Manley in the background, leading Rosie out the gate.

'Thanks a million, Johnny. Will you tell Mrs Manley I was asking for her and that I said I'm really going to miss her?'

'I will, but I suppose you won't ever call down to see us anymore now, will you?'

'Ah no, I'll be down to you all right.'

But, as it turns out, he was right.

Mam gave me a hug and asked me if I had remembered everything.

'Yeah, I have. I told you that already,' I grunted.

Within the hour, I would regret being gruff to her, the person I was going to miss the most. And, of course, she was right: I hadn't remembered everything. I had forgotten to get the bag of sixpences and the note about using the phone from her.

But that was it. It was time to leave. Marie-Thérèse ran out to the street and started waving and making faces at me. I made a face back and gave her two thumbs up out the back window. The car pulled out past Seanie Carr's house and motored down Devonshire Street and Carroll's Quay. We picked up pace along Pope's Quay, with Shandon steeple to our right and the River Lee to our left, before crossing the North Gate Bridge – and away.

I settled down, faced the setting sun and enquired, 'Is it far to Killarney?'

Postscript

In the years that followed, Johnny Creedon married Miss Healy, our shop assistant of 21 years. They were aged 54 and 37 respectively. Johnny died on 29 November 1977 and Bridgie Creedon (formerly Miss Healy) died on 16 August 2017. They are buried together at Kilquane Cemetery, Knockraha, Co. Cork. Mrs Manley died in 1986 and is also buried at Kilquane Cemetery. Mick died in 1976 and is buried at the back of Johnny's cottage.

Glossary of Terms

All-A-Bah: a children's street game in which the prize (usually a sweet) was thrown high in the air and snatched in the ensuing scuffle

Arch: bold or troublesome

Bad cess to: bad luck to, a curse

Bamin' out in dere baydinas: sunbathing in their bathing suits

Bazzer: a haircut

Bean a' tí: woman of the house

Bob: a shilling (12 pence)

Bowl-hop: one bounce of a metal bowl (pronounced 'boul' in Cork). Road bowls is a game popular in Cork, Kerry and Armagh.

Briseann an dúchas trí shúile an chait: an observation made to highlight a family trait (literally, 'The cat's pedigree/heritage will always shine through')

Caffling: messing or arguing

Cat malojen: terrible, outrageous

Cippins: small sticks used as kindling, from the Irish word *cipín*

Clatter: slap across the face

Conswilly: toilet

Cuíosach gan a bheith maiteach: average without being very bad

Dagenham Yanks: men from the Ford Motor Factory in Cork City who were transferred to the company's main works in London

Dip/plunge in the briny: a swim in the sea

Drisheen: blood sausage popular in Cork

Fatty Arbuckle: overweight Hollywood star of the silent era

FCA: Fórsa Cosanta Áitiúil (army reserve)

Fear a' tí: man of the house

Flahed out: to be exhausted

Flake: to strike or to rush

Forrum: bench

Fousterin': fussing

Guzz eye: squint

Half-crown: two shillings and sixpence; eight half-crowns to a pound

Mombolised: severely scolded

Olagóning: complaining

One, two, three, the book is read: a children's street game

Pookie pile: a dishevelled rogue

Rocker: rock

Rubber dollies: colloquial term for cheap white canvas shoes manufactured in Cork

Saecula saeculorum: for ever and ever (Latin)

Sceach: hawthorn tree or any small briary tree

Síneadh fada: the acute accent over a vowel in the Irish language

Smacht: control or discipline

Smig: face

Strop: barber's leather strap for whetting the blade of his razor

Tanner: sixpence

Tasp: energy (from the Irish *teaspach*: high-spiritedness)

Ten bob: 10 shillings (20 shillings in a pound)

The berries: excellent

The quarter sessions: a feast of food fit for a judge presiding over court sessions

Acknowledgements

I would like to thank everyone who helped in the making of this book.

To the team at Gill Books for their undimming support and belief in me. Namely, Teresa Daly, who first assured me that my story was worth telling, and worth telling in my own way; Catherine Gough, whose overview of the project was invaluable, particularly when putting the jigsaw pieces of the story together; and Aoibheann Molumby, my ever-supportive editor for her gentle way and for affording me the spaciousness to be myself throughout the entire process.

It's often said that it takes a village to raise a child; however, my immediate family alone is like a small city with a population too great to mention everyone individually. In fact, I'm sometimes surprised I had only two parents, but that's all I had. Connie Pa and Siobhán, you are the yin and yang of this boy's heart. I am so grateful for the love and laughs shared with my eleven siblings, four daughters, eight grandchildren and numerous aunts, uncles, cousins, colleagues, friends and neighbours. Thank you.

Life is a lottery, and just like my father before me, all my numbers came up on the day of my birth when I landed in Ireland. Had I any choice in the matter, it's the country I would have picked anyway.

Cork will forever be my first girlfriend, so there will always be a special place in my heart for her and for all the people I have encountered on my journey.

Above all else, I need to acknowledge the love and support of Mairéad Heffernan, who forfeited candlelit dinners for nights topping up the midnight oil on my desk as I hammered away through weekends and holidays. Thank you for all the hours of research, fact-checking and patience.

I thank every person who reads this book now and in the future. I wish you well in life's donkey derby, and whatever you do ... are you listening to me now? Do ... not ... fall ... off.

N
W
E
S
My school
Blackpool Church
Shandon Street
North Cathedral
Shandon Steeple
Leitrim Street
Lower John Street
Ned Flynn Blacksmith
Broguemakers Hill
Formica Bar
Devonshi
Carroll's Quay
Pope's Quay
North Channel
Camden Quay
Coal Quay
Cork Opera House
KILLARNEY
INCHIGEELAGH
ADRIGOLE